LATINO DROPOUTS IN RURAL AMERICA

Latino Dropouts
in Rural America

Realities and Possibilities

Carolyn Hondo
Mary E. Gardiner
Yolanda Sapien

STATE UNIVERSITY OF NEW YORK PRESS

Published by
State University of New York Press, Albany

© 2008 State University of New York

Printed in the United States of America

For information, contact State University of New York Press, Albany, NY
www.sunypress.edu

Production by Ryan Morris
Marketing by Michael Campochiaro

Library of Congress Cataloging in Publication Data

Hondo, Carolyn, 1954–
  Latino dropouts in rural America : realities and possibilities / Carolyn Hondo, Mary E.
Gardiner, Yolanda Sapien.
    p. cm.
  Includes bibliographical references and index.
  ISBN 978-0-7914-7387-0 (hardcover : alk. paper)
  ISBN 978-0-7914-7388-7 (pbk. : alk. paper)
  1. High school dropouts—United States. 2. Hispanic Americans—Education
(Secondary) 3. Rural children—Education (Secondary)—United States. I. Gardiner,
Mary E., 1953– II. Sapien, Yolanda, 1953– III. Title.

LC146.5.H66 2008
373.12'91308968073—dc22

2007025407

10 9 8 7 6 5 4 3 2 1

For Latino youth, whose stories are given in the hope we will all find it in our hearts to create ways to include them in the educational process.

To Silvia, Cristina, Maria, Beatriz, Sophia,
Armando, Cesar, Victor, and Enrique.

Many things we need can wait. The child cannot.
Now is the time his bones are being formed;
His blood is being made; his mind is being developed.
To him we cannot say tomorrow. His name is today.
Gabriela Mistral (2003)

Contents

Preface

GETTING ON AND OFF THE YELLOW SCHOOL BUS

Yolanda's father had a saying: *Quieres tapar el sol con un dedo.* The translation is, "You are trying to hide the sun with a finger." It is a Mexican *dicho*, or saying, which means you can't hide the truth for long. You can put your finger in front of your face to hide the sun, but the sun doesn't stay hidden for long. This is a metaphor for the many ways schools hide their dropouts and go through the motions of not leaving kids behind. The truth is they are leaving kids behind. The dropouts themselves can be hidden for a time, but the dropout rates cannot. Although there is some variation in the reported dropout rates, the fact that the dropout rate is very high is not disputed. About 20% of all high school students in the United States drop out of school,

> representing close to 40 percent of students in the nation's lowest socioeconomic group but also 10 percent of young people from families in the highest two socioeconomic status levels . . . The dropout problem hurts black and Hispanic communities more than others. This is because black and especially Hispanic youth are overrepresented in the lowest income groups while whites are underrepresented in these groups." (Almeida, Johnson & Steinberg, 2006)

In 2004, 40% of all high school dropouts aged 16 to 24 were Latino (Child Trends Data Bank, 2006).

Most parents hold the expectation that their child will achieve success in school, at least initially. Children all across the United States await the day they, too, can step on that yellow school bus. The road from kinder-garten to high school graduation is part of American culture. Whether or not they graduated themselves, parents do not want their child to be a high school dropout. Latino parents from low-income families are no exception, and repeatedly tell their children about the importance of education. Parents breathe a sigh of relief as their own child steps across that threshold, wearing cap and gown. Whatever else happens along the road of life "at least they graduated high school."

None of the nine students in this study graduated from high school. They are Americans and have attended U.S. schools from kindergarten through high school. They, too, initially anticipated high school graduation and dreamt of exciting careers. But, something went wrong during their middle and high school years. All of them dropped out of high school. They no longer traveled on the yellow school bus, known in high school student parlance as the "loser cruiser," a label that clearly delineates the "haves" who drove to school and the "have-nots" who needed to catch a ride, walk, or ride the bus.

The newly amended and reauthorized Elementary and Secondary Education Act (ESEA) began affecting the lives of public school educators, students, and parents in the fall of 2002. According to this federal law, renamed the No Child Left Behind Act of 2001, by the school year 2013–2014 every student in the United States will be proficient in reading, language arts, math, and science. NCLB has five main goals: accountability for results, local control and flexibility, expanded parental options, scientific research-based curriculum and decision-making, and improved teacher and parapro-fessional quality. The No Child Left Behind Act (NCLB) also requires states and school districts to improve high school graduation rates in all student subpopulations, including the economically disadvantaged, English language learners, ethnic groups, and special education students. Yet the dropout rate for Latino/a youth has continued to rise and is much higher than the rates for Whites in both urban and rural areas (Fry, 2003; Lichtenstein, 2003; Orfield, 2004; Swanson, 2003). Researchers have used mostly quantitative methods to study the problem and have studied mainly urban areas. Ladson-Billings (2006, p. 3) made the plea for more research on "What accounts for the high levels of school dropout among urban students." The experiences of Latina/o dropouts living in rural communities also need to be heard. This book gives voice to their stories. We listened to the stories of why they dropped out of school, what their lives were like in school and in their rural communities, and their views on the impact of the No Child Left Behind Act (2002).

We use the term dropout, but our position is that students are encour-aged to leave school early by an unresponsive school environment that fails to meet their needs. Of the Latina/os in our study, two of them were born in the United States of immigrant Mexican parents; the other seven were born in Mexico and immigrated to the United States as young children. For all of them the United States is their home.

The youth in this study referred to themselves interchangeably as American, Mexican, Hispanic, or Latino/a. We struggled with the right identity terminology to use for the participants because Latino cultures may vary and distinct terms are used by various groups of Mexicans in different times and places. Many terms are used in the literature and people may have multiple positioning and hybrid identities in society (Conchas, 2006; Garcia, 2006). We decided in the end to use the term Latina/os (interchanged with Latino/as so as not to favor one gender over the other), although we were cautious not to generalize about Latino/as and instead provided details on our unique participants and what they did, thought, and desired. As Tiedt and Tiedt (2005) noted, not all Latina/os speak Spanish; Latina/os can be "white, black, Indian or any mix of these; their culture and customs also vary according to the country they have come from" (p. 24). Latina/os can also be Mestizo (a cultural identity that is a blend of indigenous and European influences) and may come from Mexico, Columbia, Peru, Cuba, Honduras, Haiti, Puerto Rico, Guatemala, Guyana, Venezuela, Argentina, or other countries.

All the students in our study appeared to be capable of achieving success in school and graduating. Three students in this study had already passed all the NCLB-mandated state graduation tests; three others had passed two of three sections; and three had experienced success in elementary school and in the subjects in middle and high school that interested them. Their decisions to leave school were connected with seeking personal satisfaction and reducing the social-psychological pain of schooling. These Latina/o students did not feel valued in the schools. For instance, Beatriz said, "Our class was just a bunch of Mexicans. She [fundamentals of Math teacher] hated our class." Enrique put it this way: "Schools treat Hispanics differently." Furthermore, all the schools used a "color-blind" approach that allegedly treated all students equally, but in fact devalued the students' linguistic, cultural, and familial backgrounds.

The "color-blind" approach was not working. All of the schools had been labeled (according to NCLB guidelines) as failing the required Adequate Annual Yearly Progress (AYP) and as needing improvement. The areas of deficiency were in the English Language Learners (ELL) and low socioeconomic categories (ECON). Principals and teachers tended to blame Latina/o students in general for the school's failing status rather than examine their own teaching or explore why this was happening. The schools did not employ specific strategies to foster family connections with schools, even though this is a requirement of NCLB. It cannot be pure coincidence that in the rural alternative high schools we studied, the vast majority of students were Latino/a. Six of the nine students in our study attended alternative schools. One student, Cristina, went straight from junior high to the alternative high school, yet even the alternative schools were not effective in graduating the students.

The youth you will meet in this book are not "bad," even though the experiences of several of them might be labeled "bad" (e.g., getting into fights, using drugs and selling marijuana, driving cars fast, and in one case running from the police). Some of the students did not act out in these ways and were "good" (e.g., working hard in and out of school, waiting patiently for the teacher's guidance, and helping their family members). But they all shared a school experience where they felt unappreciated. They, like people everywhere, want to be seen as good, and to be nurtured, valued, and appreciated for *who* they are. Students' anger and disconnection from school does pose challenges for educators. But the students' oppositional behaviors were preventable: these students cried out for educators to care and to connect with them.

Studies have shown the numbers, the statistics of dropouts; this book tells their stories. Like Ladson-Billings (2006), we believe that because education is an applied field we need more than basic research; we need studies that address significant issues such as school dropout rates. With early intervention these rates may decline. We conclude with an action leadership plan—based on the experiences of the students—that itemizes how educators can create culturally responsive schools to address the needs of Latina/o youth.

The names of the communities, the school districts, and schools were changed to protect the identy of all participants in this study.

Acknowledgments

Many people contributed to this book and to all of them we give our deepest thanks. First, the book relied on the awesome knowledge of Latino/a youth: they were a joy to work with and we trust that this effort results in positive outcomes in schools. Second, our families helped us through the long process of writing a book; they are acknowledged individually below. Third, numerous individuals critiqued the manuscript and made it better. David Mueller, Gisela Ernst-Slavit, Carolyn Keeler, Kathy Belknap, Keith Anderson, and Trudy Anderson read the draft manuscript in its entirety and provided excellent feedback. Mary's Summer 2006 Multicultural Diversity and Educational Leadership class critiqued chapters and related school experiences that further confirmed the need for this book. In her class, Diana Wold demonstrated Activity 1 in Appendix G. Rosie Santana carefully critiqued Chapter 7. Dr. Keith Anderson, who lives multicultural leadership and enriches the lives of all who have the good fortune to know him, contributed the professional development activity in Appendix F, read the manuscript in its entirety, and gave helpful comments.

Gisela Ernst-Slavit provided the original title of Shattered Dreams. Colleagues at the University of Idaho in Boise and Moscow provided essential support for this project by believing in its importance and encouraging its completion. Lisa Chesnel, the acquisitions editor at SUNY Press, provided essential support throughout the research and publication process. She was always encouraging and professional.

To Carolyn's family and friends

My deepest appreciation goes to family and friends who supported this quest. I am grateful especially to my husband, Gaylen, and my children, Amy,

Karlee, and Ryan. I love you more. Thanks to Melanie for her loyal friendship, for good advice, and for thinking positively. Thanks, also, to Yolanda and Mary for their hard work and dedication to the scholarly aspect of research and writing and for caring enough about the futures of Latino/a youth to see this project to fruition. ¡Sí se puede!

To Mary's family and friends

Numerous individuals, family members, dear friends, and colleagues are my constant joy. Aunty Joyce and Uncle Ron (Joyce in the hospital following a stroke): you reminded me to always remember to dance. Aunty Mollie, the teacher: You taught me to enjoy the simple things in life and to look and listen, for you never know what you might learn. Our two amazing boys, Ryan Gardiner and Kyle Mueller: You give me my optimism for the future and inspire boundless love. Your shining eyes, excited voices and energies remind me that the best things happen in family life outside of work.

My dear parents, Walter and the late Kath Gardiner: You gave me my optimism, spirit of service, and a deep love of learning. My three brothers, David, Tim, and Ben, and their families (Kurt, Allyson, Mark, and Tara Gardiner; Robyn, Erin, Mim, and Jake Gardiner; Ann, Tom, Liz, Jon, and Kristy Gardiner): You provide a strong foundation and support. Our relatives, ex-husband David Mueller, Ron and Brigitte Curry and their daughter Chandra; Donny and Wade Walters; and Andreana, Camry, and Porshia Dix: you are my much loved American family. My good friends: Reem Anani, Ariel Blair, Carolyn Keeler, Bonnie Gallant, Melanie Burtis, Marcia Smart, Keith and Jeanne Anderson, Krista Zimmerman, Karla Cameron, Marylee Dabi, Barb Prigge, Kerri Wenger, Eileen Oliver, Ernestine Enomoto, Margaret Martinez, Gisela Ernst-Slavit, and coauthors Carolyn and Yolanda: You are the bit of chocolate we all need in our life. Russ Joki and colleagues at the University of Idaho provided a strong professional support network. Most of all, I could not have contributed anything to this world—without God.

To Yolanda's family and friends

First and foremost, I would like to thank my Lord and Savior for the many blessings that He bestowed upon me. I give Him all the praise and glory for the blessings in my life. Also, I would like to thank my family, which has always taught me to look further and to go beyond myself. They are my constant source of love, my personal support, and my inspiration. Their support and patience made it possible for me to improve my life and the lives of my students. I am so thankful for my family; they are the greatest gift in my life. Te amo.

I also wish to mention two special friends who will forever hold a place in my heart. My thanks to the late Vera Price for her dedication, her perseverance, and her faith in me. She's the reason I became a teacher. And thank you to Tina Hernandez for being a great role model and teacher. The two of you have forever changed my life, and I'll never forget you.

Last but not least, I want to say thanks to my two good friends Mary Gardiner and Carolyn Hondo for their confidence in me and for believing that I had the life experience needed to participate in the book. This book and their dedication are helping to improve the lives of Latino students everywhere. I'm grateful to have had the opportunity to work with two such knowledgeable women.

CHAPTER ONE

The High School Dropout Phenomenon

CON CARIÑO Y GANAS

Jaime Escalante was able to effectively teach low-income Latino/a students in East Los Angeles. As documented in the movie *Stand and Deliver*, poor Latino/a students, from whom nobody expected much, achieved great scholastic heights. Delpit (1995), drawing on an interview with this famous teacher, provided the missing factor in the equation of why some teachers succeed where others fail. Successful teachers, like Escalante, lovingly respect and care for their students and therefore are able to motivate their students to succeed. They inspire *ganas*: "the desire to do something—to make them believe they can learn" (p. 139). The subtitle of this chapter is *Con Cariño y Ganas*, which means "with loving respect and motivation to succeed." Once students recognize caring and respect on the part of the teacher, they are motivated and willing to learn. Success will follow. In combination with a sound knowledge of subject matter, this key pedagogical talent of the teacher who knows students, their backgrounds and culture, and how to connect with them *con cariño* results in powerful learning.

In the United States, students of color are increasing in number, but their teachers and administrators are predominantly White, as exemplified in the book *White Teachers/Diverse Classrooms* (Landsman & Lewis, 2006). Today, of the 74 million children in the United States (defined by the U.S. Census Bureau as those under age 18), the ethnic groups are as follows: White 59%, Hispanic 19%, Black 15%, Asian 4%, and Other 3% (National Center for Children in Poverty, 2006, p. 1). The 41% students of color and 90% White teachers nationwide (National Education Association [NEA], 2006b, p. 1) means that some teachers may lack the cultural knowledge to connect with their students and to inspire the motivation and confidence students need to succeed. Another report (NEA, 2006a) placed the figures at 60% students of color and 90% White teachers (5). Drawing on 2003 data from the National Center for Educational Statistics, the NEA noted that "some 40 percent of all public schools have no minority teachers on staff" (NEA, 2006a, p. 5). Although there is some variation in the numbers, it is clear that there is a sizable gap between the ethnicity of students and their educators.

Howard (2006) stated the problem well in the title of his book, *We Can't Teach What We Don't Know: White Teachers, Multiracial Schools.* According to census data trends, by the year 2050 the United States will become a "nation of minorities" with less than half of the population being non-Hispanic White (G. Marx, 2002). This is already the case in California, where, currently, more than half of the students attending urban schools are members of "minority" groups (Orfield, 2001, p. 5). Latinos make up one-third of California's population of 35 million (Tiedt & Tiedt, 2005, p. 357). In the United States, 21% of elementary and high school students have at least one foreign born parent, and approximately 300 languages are spoken. Children between the ages of 5 and 17 who speak a language other than English at home total 9.8 million, with 6.9 million speaking Spanish (Israel, 2005).

Although Latino/a children represent only 19% of the total, 40% of all dropouts aged 16 to 24 were Latina/o in 2004 (Child Trends Data Bank, 2006, p. 1). The present state of affairs in which Latina/o students do not achieve in an equitable manner and subsequently drop out of school affects individuals, schools, and the larger society. Teachers and school leaders are in a powerful position to effect change by becoming more culturally responsive to meet the needs of their students. How can teachers teach when they may know little about their students' family, language, and cultural background? In Idaho, where this study was conducted, Latina/os make up 13.42% of the public school population (Idaho State Department of Education, 2006, p. 2). Nationwide, Latino/as account for 19% of the U.S. school population (National Center for Children in Poverty, 2006, p. 1). However, "Hispanics represent only 2.9% of public school teachers and 2.8% of private school teachers" (Hodgkinson & Outtz, 1996, p. 26). This will not change rapidly and so schools are clearly in need of leaders who are well prepared to be culturally responsive in their leadership.

School dropout rates in the United States are a concern for educators, policy makers, and parents. Ladson-Billings (2006) and Orfield (2004) referred to current school dropout in the United States as a "crisis" (p. 1). Despite efforts to raise the achievement level of students in this country through new programs, curriculum innovations, and sincere efforts by policy makers and educators who want to engage students, there is still a rising percentage of Latino/as who are dropping out of high school. Latino/as drop out in larger numbers than any other ethnic group (Larson & Rumberger, 1999; Lichtenstein, 2003; Mehan, 1997; Orfield, 2004; Rumberger, 2001). Statistics, such as one in two Latino/as and African Americans drop out of school, are becoming accepted (Thornburgh, 2006, p. 30). This comes at a time when prior research confirms that every element of our nation's economy requires higher levels of math and reading skills than ever before (Fry, 2003; Lichtenstein, 2003; Swanson, 2003).

Moreover, the achievement gap or disparity between subgroups of students based on ethnicity seems to be widening (Education Trust, 2003). A recent study by the National Assessment of Educational Progress (NAEP) reported by the National Study Group for the Affirmative Development of Academic Ability (2004) showed that White students scored significantly higher than Black and Latino students in 8th- and 12th-grade mathematics and science (p. 10). Only 10% of Hispanic fourth graders and 8% of African American fourth graders scored at the proficient level in writing skills, compared with 27% of White fourth graders (p. 13). A number of factors both inside and outside of schools are thought to be responsible for the achievement gap. Educators can blame the students themselves or forces outside the school (e.g., lack of funding, the No Child Left Behind Act [NCLB], parents, or poverty). Alternatively, educators can focus on those aspects that they can directly influence, including school personnel, school climate and culture, curriculum, instruction, and assessment.

Some students who drop out of school are gifted. Colangelo and Davis (2003) noted that one in five or 20% of U.S. students who drop out of high school test in the gifted range (p. 533). The students in this study were not tested for giftedness. However, they all demonstrated an ability to succeed in school, as shown by their earlier performance, by banking sections of the state test, or by passing the state exit exams outright. Gifted, average, and struggling students are all reflected in the dropout rate statistics.

Dropout rates are sometimes ignored or hidden. The NCLB policy requires all schools, districts, and states to report to the public the academic progress of all students, including high school graduation rates. This reporting is the basis for the accountability required by the education reform law. In 2006 there was still no national database on school dropout reported by subpopulations and no systematic plan to address the challenge. In 2006 school district reporting hid real dropout rates by not reporting home-instructed students and students who transferred or moved. In Idaho, for 2004, the reported *estimate* of the cohort Hispanic dropout rate was 25.14% (Idaho State Department of Education, 2005).

Analysts called into question the methods used by states and suggested that their graduation rate calculation methods portrayed a rosier, less-than-honest picture than what actually exists. "Communities cannot make progress on this issue unless they know, without a doubt, which students start 9th grade and graduate four years later, and which do not" (Education Trust, 2003, p. 5). Accurate dropout rates counted by subcategory, though, will not fix the problem. Principals, teachers, and counselors in each of these rural schools already knew which students were dropping out: Latinos and economically disadvantaged Whites. Addressing the problem starts with an understanding of what is occurring in schools that leads to students' decisions to leave school. Then, a leadership plan needs to be implemented and its success evaluated.

WHAT *IS* THE DROPOUT RATE AND WHY DOES IT VARY?

It is difficult to get accurate figures on the dropout rate. Statistical methodology, observations, interviews, and surveys have previously been employed when looking at dropouts as a whole (Kaufman, Alt, & Chapman, 2004; Orfield, 2004; Rumberger, 2001; Wehlage, 1989). Researchers have found calculating the dropout rate difficult because some students return to school, and schools and states differ in their definitions and calculation methods (Bhanpuri & Reynolds, 2003; Delgado-Gaitan, 1988; Orfield, 2004; Riehl, 1999; Swanson, 2003; Valverde et al., 2002). In Idaho, it was reported that 19% of ninth graders do not graduate from high school (Idaho Kids Count, 2005, p. 34). However, students who graduated from eighth grade but did not return to school are not counted as dropouts, therefore the dropout rates may be even higher than reported. Moreover, the State Department of Education does not provide the dropout figures by ethnicity so dropout rates are obscured. Swanson (2003, p. iii) noted that "graduation rate estimates that are heavily dependent on dropout counts should be viewed with considerable skepticism" because of the largely inadequate national system for defining and collecting this information. The NCLB Act has refocused attention on official statistics about high school graduation and dropout rates, but to date no official system is in place.

An example of how difficult it is to accurately calculate high school dropout rates was reported by DiMaria (2004). He offered a case in point from the state of Texas, where "students who cannot be accounted for are removed from the calculation of dropouts as if they never existed. Often, incarcerated students or those who have left school but are over the mandatory attendance age (16) in their high schools are not counted" (p. 21).

Riehl (1999), in a study of 250,000 students from 93 high schools, found that school discharge policies may be important factors in the dropout phenomenon. Schools, Riehl explained, may establish admission and release criteria that correspond with social or cultural expectations. If society deems it necessary to produce fewer dropouts, schools make sure that students graduate, whether or not students are performing satisfactorily. Conversely, a school may increase the number of dropouts by adopting policies, such as requiring a minimum GPA in order to play sports, but without offering tutoring or study halls.

> Based on my interviews with school personnel, it is clear that student discharge is not a strict, rule-governed process. The staff members responsible for discharging students do have a great deal of latitude in deciding who to discharge, and there may be no simple factors to explain how they arrive at those decisions. (Riehl, 1999, p. 264)

Schools could do a valuable service to Latino/a students by examining the policies and procedures used (or not used) when deciding whether a student stays in school.

WHY DO LATINO/AS DROP OUT OF SCHOOL?

A question that has been explored by many researchers is just why do Latino/a students drop out of school? Some of the usual explanations include unequal life chances and lack of belief in the achievement ideology. There is wide-spread belief in the adage "hard work brings success" that drives much of the work in schools. However, one must also look at schooling from the viewpoint of one who has worked hard at school and failed or worked hard all their lives to just get by.

> At the core of this ideology lies the belief that life chances are determined not by politics and structures of race and class privilege, but by educational achievement. Schools are sold as exit ramps out of poor communities and into the middle class. (Fine & Burns, 2003, p. 2)

Poor, hard-working, immigrant farm laborers who have not graduated from high school may not appreciate the adage. As Bolgatz (2005) so aptly put it, "Pulling oneself up by one's bootstraps is simply easier to do if you are white"

(p. 33). Anderson (2006) added that no one pulls themselves up by their bootstraps; everyone has had assistance from others. However, for Whites the assistance may be more easily gained because Whites are in positions of power and authority in our school system.

Despite the achievement ideology promulgated in our schools, individuals who realize that the connection between effort and reward are not clear-cut may make the decision not to play the game.

> No matter how the students from the lower classes respond, the dynamic of the race for jobs of wealth and prestige remains unchanged. Although a restricted number of individuals of lower and working-class origin may overcome the barriers to success, the rules of the race severely limit and constrain the individual's mobility. (MacLeod, 1987, p. 148)

Ogbu (1987) concluded that students of color have higher school failure rates because they have learned to disbelieve the folk theory about education being the ladder to success and have instead adopted an attitude of skepticism that makes it harder to accept and follow school rules and standard practices that are required for success in school. As researchers Kozol (1991, 2005) and Nieto (2004) noted, major changes must be made in school organization, climate and culture, and policies and procedures to eliminate the social, political, and economic inequities rampant in society at large. Although they studied urban schools, the rural schools we studied need the same attention.

Family factors

Other dropout predictors in the literature included children in families with frequent patterns of moving and inconsistent school attendance, stressful family circumstances, and parental attitudes toward school. Kerr, Beck, Shattuck, Kattar, and Uriburu (2003) concluded in their study of Latino/a youth and family involvement that the family is critical to the prevention of problem behaviors of Latino/a youth, and that "monitoring and familial connectedness may be equally important for deterring adolescent risk and facilitating positive youth development" (p. 562).

Latino/a students are more likely to need to be employed and contributing to family household income than their White peers, thus reducing potential educational resources (Fry, 2002). Family socioeconomic factors play a role in whether or not youth stay in school. Until middle school, the lines between poor and rich, White and students of color are often blurred

(Aronson & Good, 2002; Erikson, 1968). Starting with middle school, according to the students in our study, the divisions manifested themselves and with each passing year became more impenetrable until the students dropped out in high school. For Latina/o students in rural Idaho the answer to why they dropped out lies partially in the complex bureaucratic school system that favors the "haves" and neglects and disadvantages others. For instance, one of the students in our study referred to herself and her Latino/a peers as the "lesser kids" (Silvia). The answer also lies partially in the school community where Latino/a students face class and social obstacles. In rural Idaho, Latina/o students are often the minority ethnically, religiously, and economically.

School-based factors

The literature pointed to poor academic performance, negative behavior, disciplinary infractions, dysfunctional student relationships, and negative attitudes of students toward peers. Nesman, Barobs-Gahr, and Medrano (2001) found, when comparing the factors of students who remained in school and those who dropped out, significant differences in attendance rates, discipline referrals, suspensions, and grade point averages. In their focus groups with Latino/a youth, participants cited personal motivation to succeed, parental support, interest in school, and involvement in school activities as crucial to successfully completing school. Other important contributing factors were supportive school staff and a clean and safe school environment. Our study both confirmed and extended their findings.

Some researchers believed that key indicators of future dropouts can be detected as early as first grade (Lockwood & Secada, 1999). The students in our study did well in elementary school and held expressed aspirations for professional careers, including attending college. Yet we found that by the end of ninth grade, these Latina/o students were becoming aware that they would not have enough credits to graduate with their peers and this awareness, coupled with negative experiences in school, helped tip the scale for them in the decision to quit.

Most researchers agreed that retention is one of the leading indicators of eventual school dropout, and some groups are retained more often than others. Hodgkinson & Outtz (1996) found that Latino/a students had been retained at least one grade more often than non-Hispanics. Hauser (2000) found that nationwide for students aged 15–17, retention rates for Black and Hispanic students are 40%–50%, compared with 35% for White students. The Jimerson, Anderson and Whipple study (2002) showed that students who are retained once are 40% to 50% more likely to drop out than promoted students (p. 452). Romo and Falbo (1996) reported that individuals do not recover from grade retention and often dropout because, "the movement toward graduation is too slow" (p. 28). Latina/o youth do not want to be 20 and graduating from high school, and schools do not want youth of that age mixing with younger students.

Compounding factors

Most researchers agreed that the dropout problem is indeed complicated, with no one clear reason for dropout cited by students in surveys (Astone & McLanahan, 1994; Hess, 2000; Rumberger, 1995, 2001; Schwartz, 1995; Wehlage, 1989). In the quest to improve the educational environment for Latino/a youth, and ultimately their chances for success in school, it is important to take a look at all the compounding factors that contribute to school dropout rates. After all, Latino/a youth do not just wake up one morning and decide not to continue with school; there is a process of dropping out that has been documented. "Dropping out is not a random, casual act . . . dropping out is the logical outcome of the social forces that limit Hispanics' role in society" (Lockwood & Secada, 1999, p. 2).

We argue that dropping out is also a result of many factors within the school environment. We decided to look at the students' schooling experiences in three rural communities to see what we could learn. The purpose of the study was to explore and describe, from the perspective of Latina/o high school dropouts from rural communities, the meaning attached to the act of leaving school, as well as the motivation for and process of dropping out. From their words we hoped to bring understanding to the phenomenon of high dropout rates for Latino/a youth because reform measures to date have done little to enhance Latina/o students' desire to stay in high school. We also developed a plan for culturally responsive leadership that arose from hearing the students' experiences.

DEFINING CULTURALLY RESPONSIVE
TEACHING AND LEADERSHIP

Culturally responsive teaching is: "an approach that empowers students intellectually, socially, emotionally, and politically by using cultural referents to impart knowledge, skills and attitudes. The use of cultural referents in teaching bridges and explains the mainstream culture, while valuing and recognizing the students' own cultures" (Education Alliance, 2006, p. 3). Establishing a culturally responsive school or district demonstrates to students and their families that they matter and that their learning matters. With early intervention for culturally responsive schooling, the dropout rates may decline. School leaders have a critical role in this effort.

School leaders must work toward four key aspects of leadership. First, they should be *multicultural leaders*, whereby they ensure that diverse students are served by their public schools with policies and practices that are multicultural. This is not just a matter of fairness and equity; it is an educational matter. As Smith (2002) found in his study, test scores rose when the focus was on an enriched educational environment that valued students' families and their cultural and linguistic knowledge. Students learn when they are safe, affirmed, and appreciated (Nieto, 2004). In addition, all students benefit from an education that promotes and values diversity by exposing students to different ideas, experiences, perspectives, and worldviews that they will need to compete and succeed in a multicultural and global society (Adam, 2006). Second, administrators should be *instructional leaders* who use their knowledge and understanding of teaching to influence how teachers teach and how students learn. Again, they need to be able to ensure culturally responsive curriculum, pedagogy, and assessment in the school and be able to raise test scores for all groups of students. Third, they should work as *managerial leaders* who manage the school finances, facilities, personnel, and compliance with the law. Creating a safe school environment is central to this work. Finally, administrators should be *participatory leaders*, whose job it is to incorporate parents, community, and other constituents into the school so that the school, as a public entity, is responsive to the public. See Appendix D for a representation of how multicultural and culturally responsive leadership tasks can be incorporated.

Principals who are culturally responsive are able to (a) incorporate multicultural knowledge and appreciation in the school; (b) raise test scores for all, including those groups traditionally underserved by public schools; and (c) engage parents and communities in the school setting. Gardiner and Enomoto (2006), drawing on Riehl's (2000) tasks for effective leadership, identified questions that administrators might ask themselves:

> The first task is fostering new meanings about diversity. For example, do principals maintain high expectations for all while providing support for diverse groups of students? To what extent do they attempt to institute and sustain school reform? How do they support dialogue and discussion among groups that might be culturally different? The second task involves promoting inclusive instructional practices within schools by supporting, facilitating or being a catalyst for change. To what extent do principals demonstrate instructional leadership that promotes inclusion, awareness of

pedagogical practices, or concern for appropriate assessments? The third task relates to building connections between schools and communities. Are principals engaged with parents and families to encourage success for their children? Do they encourage community involvement and partnering with social service agencies? To what extent do they endeavor to bridge cultural clashes between diverse groups within their school-communities? These tasks are grounded in the values of multicultural education, advocating for cultural pluralism and honoring difference while ensuring social justice and equity among all students. As such they offer a useful means to frame what is meant by multicultural leadership and how to consider its enactment. (p. 562–563)

OVERVIEW OF THE BOOK

This book complements the research and writing done by others on multicultural education, culturally responsive schools, and the creation of a school climate of caring and success for all students (see J. Banks, 2006; J. Banks & C. Banks, 2001; Capper, 1993; Delgado Gaitan, 2006; Delpit, 1995; Delpit & Dowdy, 2003; Fine & Burns, 2003; Gay, 2000; Gollnick & Chinn, 2006; Gonzales, Huerta-Macias, & Villamil Tinajero, 2002; Henze, Katz, & Norte, 2002; Ladson-Billings, 1994a, 1994b, 1995; Obiakor, 2006; Ovando & McLaren, 2000; Riehl, 2000; Robbins, R. Lindsey, D. Lindsey, & Terrell, 2002; Schmidt & Ma, 2006; Wlodkowski & Ginsberg, 2003). Where this book breaks new ground is in its attention to rural Latina/o youth dropouts, a largely invisible population in the dropout, multicultural, and social justice literature. The phenomenological method of presenting in-depth dropout experiences also complements other studies on dropouts that are literature reviews or have relied on quantitative methods.

The rural schools in this study demonstrated little recognition of the diversities of the students and families. The schools were not multicultural in their climate and culture, pedagogy, curriculum and assessment, and policies and practices, although the student bodies were diverse. Carter (2005) who conducted an ethnographic study of students in Yonkers, New York, also made this point: "Students . . . observe that educators privilege the styles, tastes and understandings of White, middle-class students, and they feel that their teachers deny the legitimacy of their own cultural repertoires and even their critiques of the information that they are expected to learn" (p. 10).

The Latina/o students in the Idaho schools in this study did not feel valued by the schools they attended. This led them to feel marginalized and to act out in ways that further marginalized them. Ultimately, they dropped out of school because it was an unrewarding experience for them. Students felt either unimportant and invisible (Maria, Sophia) or they felt that teachers and administrators openly disliked them (Silvia, Beatriz, Cristina, Cesar, Armando, Enrique, Victor). Each student was able to name from one to three teachers throughout their entire schooling experience who had cared for them, but the effects of the larger environment of uncaring negated the positive effects of these few caring teachers. These youth clearly articulated the characteristics that they sought in a good teacher: someone who was not just putting on a "front" but who genuinely cared for and respected students and their cultural and linguistic background, and who held high expectations of their ability to learn. A teacher also had to make learning "useful" and foster academic achievement.

The findings of this study are for administrators, teachers, parents, researchers, and policy makers. This phenomenology described the personal experience of being a Latina/o dropout in the context of the implementation of the No Child Left Behind Act (2002). The NCLB Act requires accountability for educators in the form of testing of students to gage proficiency but does not help educators know how to create a culturally responsive school that will enhance accountability. Educators want their students to be successful but do not always know how to gain the necessary cultural knowledge they need to help thier students. Information regarding the phenomenon of dropping out is needed to understand influences that may not be evident in test results or organizational structures. Personal, in-depth perspectives are needed on the dropout experience if the United States' public schools are to make good on the promise to leave no child behind.

ORGANIZATION OF THE BOOK

Chapter 1 provides an introduction to the study. Chapter 2 introduces the three authors and the research methods. Further details on the phenomenology and the interview guides are included in the Appendixes A and B. Chapter 3 describes the Idaho context where the study was conducted and the rural communities and schools from which the students dropped out. Chapters 4 and 5 present the personal experiences of nine Latino/a students who dropped out of U.S. rural high schools. In most cases, the students transferred to alternative high schools that served to keep them in school for a few additional weeks or months—but these schools, too, were unsuccessful in graduating the students. Chapter 6 presents thematically the study's findings and conclusions. Chapter 7 presents a leadership plan for culturally responsive schools for administrators, teachers, and counselors who want to enhance the Latino/a graduation rate and improve the educational environment for all students. School leaders can adapt these plans to their own school settings. Appendixes C, D, E, and F provide additional resources on culturally responsive schooling.

CHAPTER TWO

Research Methods

"You gotta go there to know there"
—Their Eyes Were Watching God
by Zora Neale Hurston

As an interpretive phenomenology, this study relies on the data collection and analyses of the researchers; hence, we begin with an account of the experiences and perspectives that we bring to the study. We are all educators. Carolyn taught elementary and junior high school for 26 years and has recently accepted a position as a principal of a rural elementary school. She is seeking to transform the learning opportunities for Latina/o students and students from low-income families. Mary taught in public schools in Australia for 11 years, and has served as either administrator or professor over the past 16 years in two research universities in the United States. She has created courses such as Multicultural Diversity and Educational Leadership and works to bring an ethic of care and appreciation for diversity into research, teaching and leadership. Yolanda is currently an ESL teacher in a rural high school, a position she has held for the past 13 years. She also has worked at the Newcomer Center, assisting new immigrants from Mexico in their transition into U.S. schools and society. Each of us brings a unique perspective to the writing of this book. We each have our own story to tell and our own reasons for being interested in this study. Although we seek to illuminate the lives of the young people in our study, our accounts are still partial and, at times, obscuring. Here is our attempt to help frame for the reader some of our values, interests, and purposes that we have brought to the research endeavor.

Carolyn

As a White mother of three Japanese American children, I have developed sensitivity to the issues surrounding a child's perception of acceptance and rejection in a small rural community and at school. As a teacher I worked particularly hard to help my Latina/o students by offering after-school tutoring, designing instruction to meet students' needs, and making personal contacts with parents and grandparents. It is important to develop a personal relationship with students; they really don't care how much you know until they know how much you care. Yet over years of teaching, I observed students who dropped out and wondered what I could have done differently. Many of my Latina/o students who later dropped out had difficult home situations and/or learning disabilities, but some did not seem to have any major disadvantages preventing school success. One could reasonably argue that every human has obstacles to overcome and that many people with enormous odds against them somehow manage to succeed. Freire (2001, 2004) believed that only by starting from the here and now could people begin to move forward, but people must perceive their situation, not as unalterable, but as challenging, for this to happen. Maxine Greene (1995) agreed:

> There are always pressures; there is always a certain weight in the lived situation—a weight due to the environment, to traumas from the past, or to experience with exclusion or poverty or the impacts of ideology. We achieve freedom through confrontation with and partial surpassing of such weight or determinacy. We seek this freedom, however, only when what presses down (or conditions or limits) is perceived as an obstacle. Where oppression or exploitation or pollution or even pestilence is perceived as natural, as a given, there can be no freedom. Where people cannot name alternatives or imagine a better state of things, they are likely to remain anchored or submerged (1995, p. 52)

Of course it is not all about the individuals having dreams and possibilities; it is also about schools setting up the conditions for success. The students in this study initially wanted to be doctors, teachers, and airplane pilots, but they left school without graduating and became either unemployed or working for minimum wage.

Recent attention to the immigration debate has really made me consider how differently the whole immigration debate/walkout/protest could have been handled by schools around the country. Some schools chose to lock their students in rather than let them voice their opposition or support. In many rural towns the ugly head of racism has shown itself in newspapers and in coffee shops. Legal and illegal immigrants are criticized. Few people ask why someone would risk so much to come here. Too few try to imagine the lives of others. It is such a sad state of affairs when we finally get kids to feel passionate about something and then shut them down because we fear "chaos" (to quote a school administrator in Arizona). Involvement in this study solidified for me the importance of the role of educators in building a community of learners who value and appreciate the differences and gifts of all students. As a nation, diversity is our strength.

Mary

In one way, I am a "gringo" as a White immigrant to the United States from Australia, and am aware that I can never speak for the Latina/o students in our study. But I am more importantly a social justice advocate who uses my gifts as a researcher and writer to serve those who are often forgotten in our schools: the poor of all ethnicities, Latina/os, American Indians, African Americans, and rural students. Researchers have produced well-developed literature on racism, classism, sexism, and homophobia, but we do not even have a word for rural disadvantage—would it be urbanism? Surely, rural schools have received little attention. Rural residents grow our food yet do not deserve an equally funded education? Rural students struggle, particularly when classism, racism or sexism are added to the equation. I want every piece of research to make a difference in someone's life and to make the world a better place. These are big dreams, but although I am somewhat reserved in my personality, my dreams are not so shy.

As an adolescent, like many teenagers, I was rebellious and had several years where I exhibited "bad" behavior. I was interested primarily in peer friendships, which meant exhibiting behavior oppositional to authority: smoking, talking back, not studying, questioning everything. I was in trouble at school and resented my parents. I could have become pregnant and dropped out of school, like some of the participants in this study. Although my father had dropped out of school at age 12 to work on his father's farm, my parents saw education as valuable, even for me, the girl in the family, at a time when girls' education was not highly valued in our small rural community. Also, my mom had graduated from high school so I could look to her example. I credit my eventual success in school to my parents' insistence that I succeed, an education that was relevant but not limiting, and my own desire to escape what I saw as the confines of a rural life.

Despite my background as a relatively poor White farm girl in Australia, I enjoyed White privilege and received an excellent education that benefited me. None of my teachers sought to have me leave my home culture at the classroom door; instead it was the foundation of the curriculum. All students deserve the consideration to be known and appreciated for who they are and the languages and background they bring to school. Education is important for it gave me a way out of the rural community into which I was born. Education has given me options and an ability to travel, immigrate to the United States, confront injustices, and to be heard.

Today I am mother to two boys aged seven and nine, one of whom is African American and who has had some experiences in Idaho schools that I wish he had not had. Some teachers have had low expectations for him in both academic and behavioral areas; one teacher suggested the other kids "feared" him. Another teacher asked us when she first met us whether there were any "behavioral problems" (assuming, I presume, that he would have some). He was told he had "poopy skin" in kindergarten by a girl who didn't want to sit next to him and was called "dark chocolate" by others. In line in the third grade, his friends "jokingly" said, "No Blacks allowed." Even now, his largely White classmates constantly touch his hair. Our son's experiences have made me feel hurt and angry. We struggle as a family to ensure that Ryan is enriched by and proud of his cultural heritage even while fighting day-to-day incidents and situations that present challenges.

Recently I became a U.S. citizen after many years as a permanent resident. At my own citizenship ceremony there were 137 new Americans from 31 countries; about half of the new Americans in this ceremony were from Mexico. America is the great experiment in that regard; no other country has so much cultural, linguistic, or religious diversity. The diversity of the United States has made it great with all the talent and energy and new ideas of many countries. I believe the United States can be even greater if we educate all of our citizens to be caring citizens of the world. We are only as strong as we care for all individuals; as my friend Keith Anderson so aptly puts it, we all belong to the human race.

For many years I was a teacher and for two years, an administrator. I know what teaching and administration demands and how little society seems to appreciate the service and self-sacrifice of the teaching profession. For the administrators, teachers, and counselors for whom this book is written, please take the critique of policies and practices in the spirit in which it is intended: not to attack or destroy, but to teach and offer a new perspective derived from the rural Latina/o students' experiences and from the researchers. This book is one small effort to contribute to education that is inclusive and relevant to all those in our multilingual, multicultural society. There is nothing White about education; education and opportunity are for everyone.

Yolanda

I was born in El Paso, Texas, to Cruz and Magdalena Martinez. My parents were both migrant field workers with little or no education. I'm the oldest of six. We migrated to Idaho when I was five years old. As a migrant child, life wasn't easy. I remember spending my childhood moving back and forth between small, segregated towns in Idaho to Nebraska, the Dakotas, California, and Minnesota. We went where the jobs were. I remember my parents picking tomatoes, beans, onions, cherries, grapes, apples, and plums, and hoeing beets from sunrise to sunset. The life of the migrant worker was hard. Most of the work was "stoop labor." That meant my parents had to bend over all day to pick the crops and got paid very little.

Meanwhile, my sisters and I either stayed in the car and listened to our favorite cumbias or played in the dirt and made mud pies. I remember the rows of beans in Wisconsin were longer than the sugar beets rows in Minnesota. When there were long rows, my parents would let my sisters and me be in the field with them instead of waiting at the edge of the field with the water bucket.

I didn't attend school continuously because I had to watch my two little sisters. And anyway, education wasn't a priority to my parents; their philosophy was that I didn't need an education to be a housewife. After the harvest was done, we would return back to Idaho, to the same labor camp, the same grungy two-room apartment, and the same school. I never understood my father's decision to seek migratory work. But we were a poor Mexican American family, and it became a familiar routine. This lifestyle continued until my parents received jobs at a local food processing plant called J. R. Simplot.

As long as I can remember, school was such a threat to me. In school I learned that I was different. I learned that I was poor, I dressed funny, I spoke funny, I smelled funny. I was treated as an illegal immigrant, even though I wasn't; I was an American just like my classmates. My sister and I were segregated until I was in the fifth grade and she was in the fourth grade. Mexican children were placed in a special education classroom until they learned the English language. In school, I became withdrawn and kept to myself. I never made any friends. I was never asked to participate in any other school activities because I didn't speak English. My grades were Ds and Fs and I was retained and I didn't care. I begged and pleaded with my father to take me out of school because I wasn't learning anything anyway. I was not comfortable in school. Teachers were hostile toward me, and the administrators routinely disregarded my most basic needs. Real learning is difficult to sustain in an atmosphere rife with mistrust. Nobody cared. After years of frustration and failure, I dropped out in the eighth grade.

In 1969, at the age of 15, I met and married my husband Pedro. At 16, I was a mother. I stayed in town and made tortillas every day, tamales at Christmas, menudo on Saturday, and *barbacoa* on Sunday morning. At the time, I believed this was my obligation as a woman. My great grandmother did it, my grandmother did it, my mother did it, and now, it was my turn.

I was living the life that was expected of me. It is especially hard for girls whose parents are from the first generation born in the United States.

My parents expected no more of me than to be a local Mexican girl who married a local Mexican guy and became a *mamacita*, a *tia*, a *comadre*, and finally, an *abuelita*.

For years, I was happy being a mother and wife. I cannot recall when I started to want more. In 1988, I worked toward my GED. At first I was scared. School was never easy for me. I spoke English poorly. But I had two very special teachers who became my mentors. They encouraged, coached, praised and believed in me. Before I realized it, I was enrolled with 12 credits at CSI, the College of Southern Idaho. I graduated with an associate degree and then took my next big step to a university. I didn't know where I was headed. I just knew that I had developed a passion for learning. I graduated with a Bachelor of Arts in Elementary Education from Idaho State University.

In 1993, I got a job teaching ESL, English as a Second Language, at Burley High School. At the same time, I taught ESL to adults at night part-time for the College of Southern Idaho. I really enjoyed teaching adults. However, I wanted to further my education. In 2000, I decided to get my administrative (principal) certificate from the University of Idaho. Then, in 2004, I got my ESL/bilingual masters. Now, I'm working toward my Educational Specialist degree and superintendent credential from the University of Idaho. At the same time, I have still continued teaching ESL at Burley High School for the last 13 years.

Now, it is very clear to me what my passion is. It is to reach the children who are forgotten. I took a personal interest in this book because the students' testimonies brought back many memories of my own childhood struggles. I found myself reliving and sharing with these students many of the same feelings, thoughts, and reactions to the realities of their lives. Tragically, our schools lack the compassion and the will to eliminate some of these realities, which are as harsh and oppressive for the Mexican students of today as they were for me 30 years ago. My heart aches every time I hear the statistics about the Latino/a dropout rate. It is high, too high. I am not ready to abandon hope. I am not ready to see more of the hurt and disappointment in their eyes. This book will open the eyes of administrators, teachers, board members, and parents. Today more than ever, we need a teaching force that truly reflects the demographics of all students.

THE STUDY DESIGN

Given the problem of large and increasing numbers of Latina/o students dropping out of school, the purpose of this study was to utilize a phenomenological perspective to explore the experience of being a Latino/a high school dropout. Van Manen (1996) noted that phenomenology shows us what various ranges of human experiences are possible, what worlds people inhabit, how these experiences may be described, and how language (if we give it its full value) has powers to disclose the worlds in which we dwell. (p. 11)

Through the participants' responses during in-depth interviews and the researchers' reflexivity, an intimate view of the world of a Latino/a dropout is articulated.

Through our research, we wished to discover the following: What was the school experience for Latina/o high school dropouts from rural communities in the context of the No Child Left Behind Act (2002)? What was the process of rural Latina/os dropping out of school? What does it mean to rural Latina/os to leave high school prior to graduation? The interviews were designed to understand the essence of dropping out, and what and how it was experienced. The study was approved by the University of Idaho Human Assurances committee, and the researchers also completed the Human Participant Protection Education for Research Teams examination from the U.S. National Institutes of Health. See Appendix A for more on the research process and Appendix B for the interview guides. Answers to these research questions are provided in Chapters 3, 4, 5, and 6. We also sought to bring care into the research endeavor itself and consider how understanding the process of dropping out of school may provide us with new ways to effectively reach out to students. These results are presented in Chapter 7.

The study focused on students living in agriculturally based rural communities of less than 10,000 people, where there were significant Latino/a populations in the schools. The study did not include completely rural communities, defined as having a population of less than 2,000; these communities are usually predominately White in the state of Idaho where this study was conducted. Rural schools, as defined by the National Center for Education Statistics (NCES, 2007), are those located within communities of 20,000 or less; these rural communities enroll one-third of the students in America. Statistically, rural schools do not do well under NCLB's requirements for AYP (adequate yearly progress), often with failure in the subgroups of low socioeconomic status (ECON) and Latino/Hispanic population (HISP) (NCES, 2007).

SAMPLING

Individuals and sites were selected as those which "might provide useful information, might help people learn about the phenomenon, and who might give voice to silenced people" (J. W. Creswell, 2002, p. 193). Purposeful sampling was used to identify the participants, based on individuals judged to have rich experiences related to the study. Snowball sampling, a method of expanding the sample with the help of key people who are in a position to identify and recommend possible participants, was also used.

Participants were purposively selected based on the following criteria:

• Identified themselves as Latina/o, Hispanic, Mexican, or Mexican American
• Dropped out of a public school since the enactment of NCLB in 2001
• Not enrolled in an alternative school or private school, nor finished a GED program

Ethically, the researchers were committed to the idea that not only would no harm come to participants in the study, but that some good might come in the process from encouraging school completion through an alternative avenue. To show reciprocity and care in the research process, the researchers provided information on the High School Equivalency (HEP) program and strategies to attain the General Education Diploma (GED).

In order to protect the participants, each one was given a pseudonym. All names of communities were changed, as well as any other identifying characteristics. Each participant and his or her parent or guardian signed the informed consent form after receiving an overview of the study and participant rights. Only participants who signed the consent form and had parental permission to participate were retained. J. Creswell (1998) recommended interviews with up to 10 people for a phenomenological study. For this study, 9 individuals were selected from three rural communities.

All the students were Americans and had attended U.S. schools from kindergarten through the beginning of high school. Eight of the nine youth came from lower socioeconomic families. One participant, Silvia, had parents who were both educated professionals. See Table 1 for details on study participants.

DATA COLLECTION

Data were collected in the 2004–05 school year, with follow-up interviews and analysis conducted over the next two years. The participants were Latino/a individuals who had dropped out of high school since 2001, following the implementation of NCLB (2002). In order to honor the privacy of persons who have dropped out of high school, teachers, counselors, school administrators, rural health-care personnel, social service personnel,

TABLE 1. THE NINE LATINO/A HIGH SCHOOL DROPOUTS

	Silvia	Cristina	Maria	Beatriz	Sophia	Armando	Cesar	Victor	Enrique
Age left school	15	17	16	17	17	19	17	16	16
Last grade	9th	9th	10th	11th	11th	9th	10th	11th	10th
High school	Hagerstown	Zaragosa Alt.	Juniper Hills	Ennis then Zaragosa Alt.	Ennis then Zaragosa Alt.	Hagerstown then Alt.	Hagerstown	Expelled from Juniper Hills then attended Alt.	Expelled from Juniper Hills then attended Alt.
Grades and tests	Good grades with IEP until high school	Poor grades after grade school	LEP; IEP; Poor grades; *Passed 2 of 3 high stakes grad. tests	Good grades until 9th grade; *Passed high stakes grad. tests	Average grades until 10th grade	Poor grades *Passed 2 of 3 high stakes grad. tests	Aver. grades;	Poor grades; *Passed high stakes grad. tests	Poor grades after 8th grade; *Passed high stakes grad. tests
School Interest	Basketball	Math Biology	Music Band	History Science	Math	Sports	Math; Soccer	Sports	None named
Childhood aspiration	Pilot	Beautician	Teacher	Lawyer	Teacher	Police officer	Mechanic	Medical doctor	Architect
Current work; Family responsibility	Three part-time jobs; baby-sitting, cleaning	No job; helps grand-mother	Works as sorter in onion/cherry sheds	Mother to 2 children; waitress	Mother to 1 child; dish-washer	Father to 1child; caretaker for sick parent	No job due to arrest on drug charges	No job; was working as a roofer	No job; was working as farm laborer in onions
No. of children	0	0	0	2	1	1	0	0	0

(continued on next page)

TABLE 1. (*continued*)

	Silvia	Cristina	Maria	Beatriz	Sophia	Armando	Cesar	Victor	Enrique
Parents' marital status	Married	Divorced	Married	Divorced	Divorced	Married	Married	Divorced	Married
Parents' jobs	Professionals	Farm laborer	Farm laborer	Farm laborer	Farm laborer	Father on disability	Farm laborer	Farm laborer	Farm laborer
Parent expectation re: school	Parents expect her to get a GED and college	Mother wanted her to finish school	Parents wanted her to finish school; support decision to work	Mother wanted her to finish school; college plans future	Father wanted her to finish school; mother wanted her to work to help family	Family has values employment over school	Supportive for college; strong work ethic	Parents wanted him to finish school or obtain GED; college	Strong support for college

and Latino/a leaders in these communities were asked to contact individuals who had dropped out of school since 2001. These people identified potential participants and asked them if they would be interested in participating in the study, and if their name and contact information could be shared. The names of those who expressed an interest in participating were then contacted personally.

Participants in the study were purposively selected individuals who had experienced the phenomenon of dropping out of high school. Participants were asked to describe the experience as they lived through it. The focus was on describing the experience from the inside, from the state of mind: the feelings, the mood, the emotions, and so on (Merriam, 2002; Van Manen, 1990).

In each community an interview site was used that protected the identity of the participant, provided a quiet location for interviews, and was easily accessible. Locations included the public library, county or city office buildings, and empty rooms at the schools, wherever the participant felt most comfortable. Although the focus was on the students' perspectives, and information from dropouts made up the bulk of the data, interviews were also conducted with teachers, administrators, counselors, juvenile probation officers, family members, and others in order to triangulate data and corroborate information. Access to the school and school personnel was gained by getting permission from district superintendents and building principals.

Interviews were conducted in English because all participants were proficient. The literature on dropouts indicated that of the 40% of Latino dropouts who are born in the United States, 95% speak English well, although some may come from homes where Spanish is the dominant language (Fry, 2003, p. 13). This study concentrated on those individuals.

Specific steps in observing, interviewing and analyzing documents from research sites were followed (J. W. Creswell, 2002; Moustakas, 1994, 1995; Worthen, 2002). Interviews were dated, and each recorded on a separate cassette with participant permission. Following each interview, memos were written regarding what transpired and reflections upon the event. These memos were also dated and coded for correlation purposes. As soon as possible after each interview, the interviews were transcribed. The interview guides are included in Appendix B.

METHODS OF DATA ANALYSIS

The first step in data analysis was bracketing our own biases and assumptions to become more aware of the voices of participants and how they might differ from our own experiences. We can have empathy and even identify with our participants and share life experiences with them, but we must also document and reflect on how those biases and assumptions might be playing into the analysis and write-up throughout the study.

Bracketing, the act of suspending one's various beliefs in order to study the essential structures of the world, is an important element in the Husserlian approach to hermeneutic, or interpretive, phenomenology. The process of bracketing in its ideal form consists of taking no positions, either for or against, and not allowing presuppositions or the researcher's own meanings and interpretations to enter the unique world of the informant/participant. Groenewald (2004) suggested that to arrive at certainty, "anything outside immediate experience must be ignored, and in this way the external world is reduced to the contents of personal consciousness" (p. 4). We think research is less certain than this. We as researchers all hold biases, assumptions, values, interests, and purposes in relation to the study. Therefore, to enhance rigor, we were as transparent as possible in our reflections of our interests and values in order to be constantly aware of our individual or collective efforts to shape the data and analysis a certain way. Throughout the analysis process, individually and as a collective, we attempted to bracket or closely examine our preconceived hypotheses, questions, or personal experiences through writing in a reflective journal and through our collaborative discussions.

With bracketing continuing throughout the study, the following steps in phenomenological data analysis, recommended by J. Creswell (1998) and Moustakas (1994), were employed. In Step 2 we read all transcriptions in their entirety many times to become familiar with the data. We then wrote narrative case studies on each student, using primarily the participant's words (Chapters 4 and 5). Significant statements (SS) were identified from each description, then listed and given equal value, a process called *horizontalization.* In Step 3 we formulated these significant statements into meanings, and these meanings were clustered into themes (CT), or units of meaning by removing overlapping and repetitive statements. In Step 4 the themes were developed into a narrative *textural* description describing the phenomenon of dropping out of school. The textural description of the phenomenon included *what* was experienced by the participants. The *structural* description included *how* the participants experienced dropping out (revealed in Chapter 6). In Step 5, also presented in Chapter 6, we wrote the exhaustive summary, or final statement, of the essence of the phenomenon; Fighting back and seeking satisfaction: A theory of dropping out. In Chapter 7 we used the findings to develop a culturally responsive leadership plan based on Latino/a experiences.

We wanted our research to both advance theory and provide practitioners with solutions to real world administrative and teaching problems. We were careful to allow the data and the students' experiences to inform the plan, rather than imposing our own ideas. In Step 6 member checking, soliciting feedback about one's data and comclusions, was conducted with six of the nine participants to validate our findings and integrate new data into our study's findings.

SUMMARY

For all three researchers the interest in multicultural issues is both personal and professional. We have a vested interest in seeing our schools become more culturally responsive. At the same time, we do not wish to disparage educators. Teachers, counselors, and principals are heroes, underpaid and often undervalued. We know that, as researchers, we do not have all the answers and that we have made and continue to make many mistakes in our own professional lives. We are not always attentive to all of our students or as responsive as we ought to be; it is easy to armchair theorize. Putting ideas into practice takes much more. We offer these accounts of high school dropouts' experiences so that administrators, counselors, teachers, and policymakers can know what it is that real students are thinking, doing, and desiring.

Only Yolanda has had the experience of dropping out of school. She is now highly educated and teaches students like the ones in this study. None of us really know what it is like today to be poor and marginalized by the school system. Yolanda comes closest as the author who has lived a life similar to the students, so she brings a critical perspective to the book. Carolyn wrote her dissertation on the topic of Latino/a dropouts (Hondo, 2005), which developed later into this book. She conducted the fieldwork, listened closely to the students' accounts and brought out the fullness of their stories. Mary kindled the interest in matters of multicultural leadership by teaching both Carolyn and Yolanda in her course, Multicultural Diversity and Educational Leadership. The course encourages teachers, counselors, and administrators to critically examine their own schools and school systems for inequities and to develop a multicultural leadership plan to address these injustices. In this book, together we tell the stories of students in six schools in rural Idaho and provide some workable approaches for us and other educators to use in working more effectively with Latina/o school students and with those from low-income families.

CHAPTER THREE

Inside Three Rural
Schools and Communities

Widely recognized for its "famous potatoes," Idaho is also known for its scenic beauty, kayaking, hunting, and fishing. Survivalists are said to live in Idaho, alongside human rights activists. (In Northern Idaho, activists managed to oust a racist neo-Nazi organization from its compound. For an account of the small-town human rights activism that helped bankrupt the White supremacist movement see Vogt, 2003). A recent newspaper article gave the following description of Idaho: "To liberals on both coasts, Idaho is redneck country, famous only for its potato industry and its White supremacists" (Gamache, 2006, p. 1). Idaho is a predominantly White state. Of the 1.3 million residents in the state approximately 89% are Caucasian; 8% Hispanic; 1.5% American Indian or Alaska Native; less than 1% African American; and less than 1% Asian American (U.S. Census Bureau, 2000). In Idaho 17.7% of children live in poverty (comparable to the U.S. national rate of 17%), and 42% of school-age children or 74,433 children receive free or reduced lunch per day (Idaho Kids Count, 2005, p. 38). According to the last census, Idaho's poverty rate was 13.9%, comparable to the national average of 13% (U.S. Census Bureau, 2000).

Technology has become the number one industry in Idaho, although Idaho is still a state with a strong foundation of agriculture (and yes, potatoes) as its economic base. Immigrant laborers support that base. Many of the immigrants in Idaho, both documented and undocumented, come from Mexico. Latino students make up 12.41% of the Idaho public school population (Idaho State Department of Education, 2006). Many of these children do not do well in school and drop out of high school. The Idaho Commission on Hispanic Affairs (2004) reported that 6,522 Hispanic youth dropped out of Idaho public high schools between the school years of 1993–4 and 2001–02. In general, an estimated 25% of Hispanic students drop out between the 9th and 12th grades (p. 51). This is not a problem just for Idaho. In the United States in 2004, 40% of high school dropouts aged 16 to 24 were Latino (Child Trends Data Bank, 2006, p. 1).

The world of Latino high school dropouts described in this book is one of rural schools where funding and access to intervention programs are limited. Poverty in rural communities is a contributing factor to the drop out rate. One study suggested that rural communities display a ubiquitous acquiescence to higher Latino dropout rates (Jordan, McPartland, & Lara, 1999). Rural populations may place less emphasis on high school graduation for a variety of reasons, social or economic. Researchers such as Hodgkinson & Obarakpor (1994) have drawn attention to the rural economic situation by contrasting it with poor metropolitan areas. Their study highlighted the disparities and lack of services in rural areas, including inequitable education, inadequate health care, and lack of access to public transportation. Rural areas also often lack access to professional jobs with higher pay (Kaminski, 1993), keeping most residents in low-skilled, low-paying positions. Lichtenstein (2003) reported that "in the past there were always decent jobs for those without strong literacy skills. Those jobs have virtually disappeared" (p. 4).

Rural schools and their administrators and teachers are also challenged by the No Child Left Behind Act (2002). NCLB holds educators accountable for improving the academic performance of every group of students, and poses a challenge for rural schools and districts that are more likely to be labeled as low performing or needing improvement. NCLB requires low-performing schools to divert 20% of Title I funds to transport students to higher-performing schools, and for supplemental educational services such as private tutoring, even though schools may need those funds to help students make academic progress (Jehlen, 2003). "The major obstacle facing rural districts is access to resources. Under current funding formulas, many rural districts do not have access to the financial resources that urban and suburban districts have" (Reeves, 2003, p.1). The financial implications of NCLB for rural schools and communities have not yet been addressed by lawmakers.

In Idaho, 15% of the elementary school population is Latino; however, only 4% of public school teachers are Latino, resulting in a significant gap between the ethnicity of students and their educators (U.S. Census Bureau, 2000). Nationwide, there is a lack of Latino educators. "Hispanics represent only 2.9% of public school teachers and 2.8% of private school teachers" (Hodgkinson & Outtz, 1996, p. 20). Mary's son, Ryan, one of two African American boys in the fourth grade at an urban elementary school of 700 students, has not yet had a Latino/a or African American teacher or administrator, and it is possible that, unless the family moves from Idaho, he may complete his school career without ever having one. Mary's students sometimes tell her, "Remember, this is Idaho. We don't have a lot of need for multiculturalism here." She replies, "Multicultural education may be even more important in Idaho since racism and intolerance can flourish where there is a perceived absence of diversity." In Idaho, no less than in other parts of the country, teachers and administrators must be knowledgeable about their diverse students. A disservice is being done to our White students, as well as our students of color, if they do not receive an education that makes them multiculturally competent and able to communicate with and appreciate a wide variety of people. This is an economic reality as well as an ethical issue. Businesses are attracted to communities with excellent schools and where diversity flourishes.

The Latino dropouts in this book live in three agriculturally based rural communities in Idaho. These communities were chosen because they had diverse populations from 2,000 to 10,000 people, with between 25% and 57% Latinos (U.S. Census Bureau, 2000). The names of these communities, the school districts, and schools were changed, and care has been taken to protect the identity of all participants in the study.

According to a recent publication of the Idaho Commission on Hispanic Affairs (2007), the Latino population in Idaho has risen by 92% since 1990. Now Latinos exceed 120,000 people, or 8.84 % of all residents, with 46% 19 years old or under, and about 41% between 20 and 44 years old (p. 11). "One of the most important issues facing Latino families in Idaho is the education of their children. Obtaining better educational outcomes for these students is vital to preserving families and to our state's prosperity" (Idaho Commission on Hispanic Affairs, p. 50). The current high Latino/a dropout rate is a concern for everyone.

COMMUNITY #1: HAGERSTOWN, IDAHO

With a population of almost 8,000, Hagerstown is the largest of the three communities in which this study took place. About 30% of the town's inhabitants are Latino (Idaho Commission on Hispanic Affairs, 2004). The median income for Hagerstown is approximately $30,000. Of the adults living in this community, aged 25 and older, 72% have graduated from high school (U.S. Census Bureau, 2000). All authority figures in the community and schools are White, and predominantly male. This quiet little community has experienced a small renaissance, an exception to the rule in rural Idaho. According to the city administrator, the community of Hagerstown is currently enjoying better economic prosperity than most in Idaho due to an influx of new industry. Hagerstown has also become a bedroom community to a larger city about 20 miles away. Most homes within the Hagerstown boundaries are older, but well-groomed. There is a sense of pride in the appearance of each yard, even in poorer neighborhoods.

Hagerstown High School

The Hagerstown school district serves approximately 3,000 students, which includes students from outside the city limits. In the district, 39% of the students have applied for the free/reduced meals program. The percentage of Latino/a students has risen steadily over the past 10 years. In 1999, 19% of the students were Latino/a. Today, a little over 25% of the students enrolled in this district are Latino/a (District Profile, 2005).

Hagerstown High School is located on the outskirts of the community. It is the newest of the school buildings in the Hagerstown school district; the other schools are decades older. With the implementation of the No Child Left Behind Act (2002), both elementary and secondary schools were, according to a district administrator, restructured to "accelerate the learning of identified at-risk students" (also see Ambrosio, 2004; Jehlen, 2003; Reeves, 2003). However, Hagerstown High School has still not met the Adequate Yearly Progress (AYP) benchmarks required by NCLB and is listed as needing improvement. The school missed the goal for the Hispanic reading proficiency (HISP), but has attained "safe harbor" status for ELL (English Language Learniner) and ECON (economically disadvantaged students). The safe harbor provision indicates an improvement over previous scores by at least 10%.

The high school does not have a formal dropout prevention program, although the alternative school is an option that some students choose. Typically, about half of the alternative school enrollment is Latina/o, but the graduation rate from the alternative school is only about 20% to 30%. According to the vice principal, the types of programs needed to provide interventions for at-risk students are not funded by NCLB. Educators feel they are doing the best they can with the taxes they receive. The vice principal did not "think the local taxpayers would be willing to have taxes increased in order to keep the marginalized, or at-risk, student in school" (personal communication, February 23, 2005). One probation officer indicated a similar lack of interest by the community in "those kids" (personal communication, February 11, 2005).

School personnel suggested a variety of methods used to encourage students to stay in school. Each year the school holds a career fair, which draws about 1,000 students from the middle school and high school. Students are introduced to representatives from over 50 organizations, including businesses, colleges, clubs, and branches of the military. All students at Hagerstown are encouraged to participate in school sports and activities, although they must meet academic standards. The high school also supports La Raza, a youth leadership program for Latina/os, and has initiated a Latina/o school newspaper. According to a county probation officer, the problem is not with students choosing to drop out; the problem is the district's inflexible attendance policy and a zero-tolerance policy that is being used to expel students for being bothersome. Some of the students who are expelled or drop out because of attendance issues shift to the district alternative school.

Hagerstown Alternative High School does not offer day care, an option found in other districts, and transportation is not provided. Fewer classes are offered than at the mainstream high school, and there is no counseling available. Many Latina/o dropouts are eligible to take advantage of the High School Equivalency Program (HEP), but are reluctant to leave their homes and families to attend the program, which is offered in the state capital.

The graduation rate from Hagerstown High School was 70% for the class of 2004. The graduation completion percentage does not include General Education Diploma (GED) or high school equivalency certificates. Ethnicity and gender rates for this percentage are not reported on the state website, and district officials will not make these numbers available. Data available from the Idaho State Department of Education (2006) on district profiles showed that approximately 6.3% of the students at Hagerstown High School, grades 9 through 12, drop out each year, an accumulated, or cohort rate of 25.2% (www.sde.state.id.us).

The Hagerstown school district has the lowest graduation rate of the three communities in this study, the fewest number of Latina/o residents and students, and the highest median income. Because the state data is not disaggregated, it is difficult to tell whether a significant number of these dropouts are Latina/o. However, every adult interviewed mentioned that many Latina/o youth in this community drop out at age 16 to work. One authority figure from the community opined that Latina/os in the community, and especially those attending the schools, are generally marginalized by most residents and seen as a "problem" that must be tolerated because of the need for farm labor.

COMMUNITY #2: JUNIPER HILLS, IDAHO

Nestled in the heart of farm country, life in Juniper Hills limps along. With the downturn in agricultural commodity prices, the economic strength of communities like Juniper Hills has weakened. Empty dilapidated buildings dot the main road. Convenience stores have replaced grocery stores, and community services are scarce. Sidewalks are rare, and those that exist are broken and crumbling. Property and homes are in poor condition, and various stages of decay and neglect are evident.

Juniper Hills has a population of almost 4,000. It is the smallest of the three communities highlighted in this study; however, about 57% of the residents are Latina/o. The median income is nearly $23,000, which is below the federal poverty level for a family of six (Idaho Commission on Hispanic Affairs, 2004). Most people who are employed work in the agricultural industry, where seasonal work is common, with winter months bringing dependence on unemployment assistance. There is no access to mass transit, so residents must either walk or drive to their workplaces. All authority figures in the community and schools are White, and mostly male. In Juniper Hills, only 46.4% of adults aged 25 and older have been awarded high school diplomas.

Juniper Hills High School

The Juniper Hills school district serves approximately 903 students, 67% of whom apply for free or reduced meals. District enrollment has remained fairly constant in the past five school years, with about 55.4% of the students listed as Hispanic. The school is within the city limits and is part of an education complex that contains all of the district's schools. The buildings are newer and in good condition, a stark contrast to the surrounding residential area. Many students walk to school; however, students are also bussed from outlying areas of the county. Juniper Hills High School has not met the AYP proficiency benchmarks required by NCLB for reading, math, or language.

Juniper Hills has an alternative school that is several miles from town. Students who attend provide their own transportation. At the Juniper Hills Alternative School, students can take two courses each trimester. Most often students are referred to the alternative school if they have not accumulated enough credits to graduate in the regular school program, if they have issues with attendance, or if they have violated the district zero-tolerance policy. The policy imposes suspension from the regular high school program for infractions related to weapons, drugs, criminal activity, or "aggressive behavior."

Juniper Hills High School does not have a formal dropout prevention plan, but educators are attempting to initiate a mentoring program despite sparse community involvement. "Teachers take an interest in individual students and this seems to be our best informal method (of dropout prevention) at this time" (school administrator). With the NCLB Act, the school adopted more stringent guidelines for attendance, and focused more on students who needed English language skills. The principal mentioned that student athletes undergo grade checks every three weeks. If student athletes are failing any class, they become ineligible to play until the next three week's check. Often students are ineligible for most of the season.

The graduation rate from Juniper Hills High School was 74% for the class of 2004. In a personal interview, one district employee explained that "these kids do not see dropping out as a bad thing. We're working on changing that, but there is still a long way to go." The graduation completion rate does not include GED or high school equivalency certificates. Ethnicity and gender rates for this percentage were not disaggregated for this site. Data available from the Idaho State Department of Education on district profiles showed that approximately 6.1% of the students, grades 9 through 12, drop out each year, for an overall rate of 24.7%. Because the data are not disaggregated by ethnicity, it is difficult to ascertain whether a significant number of these dropouts are Latino/a.

Teachers working in the Juniper Hills school district spoke about their discomfort with the pressures of NCLB requirements on small schools. One teacher remarked that they have all worked "really hard" to improve the Latino/a student population's achievement levels. According to her, the Limited English Proficient (LEP) students are named as "the ones most likely to drop out because they cannot pass the 10th grade Idaho Standards Achievement Tests (ISAT)." She confided that the principal said that "maybe they shouldn't work so hard to keep these kids in school" because when they stay their ISAT scores put the school in failure status. "Maybe we should just let them go," the employee concluded. The teacher affirmed the district employee's dedication to the school and to students, "but outside pressures to show proficiency are tremendous" (personal communication, January 31, 2005). In the literature this phenomenon is referred to as "push out," signifying the pressure of school officials on students to leave school early (Jordan et al., 1999; Orfield, Losen, Wald, & Swanson, 2004; Reeves, 2003).

Lack of adequate funding was mentioned by administrators and teachers as one of the biggest impediments to meeting NCLB goals. Of the three communities in this study, Juniper Hills has the lowest population, lowest median income, and the highest percentage of Latino residents and students. Almost half of the adults in the community did not graduate from high school, but the high school is now graduating about 71% of its seniors.

COMMUNITY #3: ENNIS, IDAHO

Despite community attempts at revitalization, and advertising pleas to "shop at home," the local businesses in Ennis barely get by on the small number of regular shoppers. Empty storefronts point out the economic reality of rural communities in the new millennium. The population of Ennis, currently just over 5,500 people, has steadily declined in the past five years, taking with it property values and tax revenues. The median income is a little over $25,000, which is below the federal poverty level for a family of six (Idaho Commission on Hispanic Affairs, 2004). The majority of Ennis residents are White; 38.9% are Latino/a. All authority figures in the community and in the schools are White, and predominantly male. Agriculture is the main enterprise of this area, and most Latino/as are employed as farm laborers or in factories that process farm commodities (Idaho Commission on Hispanic Affairs, 2004). There is no mass transit, so residents either walk or drive to work. In Ennis, 65.3% of adults aged 25 and older graduated from high school.

Ennis High School

The Ennis school district has a little over 4,000 students, including students from the outlying areas of the county. The free or reduced meal program is utilized by 52% of the students in the district. The schools are in a declining state, and no new schools have been built for over 10 years; however, a bond proposal to remodel the high school passed successfully. Because of the passage, Ennis High School has been updated to include technology, science labs, a new library, and an additional gymnasium complex. The high school is located outside of the city limits, and students either ride a school bus or drive to school.

According to a county probation officer, there is strong support by juvenile justice officials in Ennis County to keep kids in school. Students who are removed from school because of the zero-tolerance policy are required to either attend alternative school or to work on the GED. This officer mentioned that the high school pushes out kids who are academically challenged, but works to keep troubled kids who scored well on the ISATs. "The school would call and make sure high-scoring kids will be in school for the ISAT testing days" (personal communication, March 17, 2005).

While assisting in the search for interview participants, the high school administrator could not specifically name a Latino/a individual or recall conversing with anyone who might have fit the needs of this study. When asked about the possibility of asking a school counselor, the principal said that they would probably not be helpful. "They spend a lot of time with scheduling and when they do counseling it is mainly career counseling, you know, for kids that need help getting into college. We really don't see our high school counselors getting into the personal lives of most students. And if there are discipline issues, the vice principal takes care of it" (personal communication, January 15, 2005).

However, a referral to the Zaragosa Alternative High School principal opened the door to Latino/a high school dropouts from the Ennis school district. Zaragosa Alternative High School is named by interview participants as a caring and inviting environment. The school holds two different classes each trimester, and students are dismissed at 1:30 pm. The early release enables students to attend physical education or other courses that are available only at Ennis High School. No electives are offered at Zaragosa. Transportation is an issue, however, as it is not provided and students have to find their own way from Zaragosa to Ennis High School, which is several miles away. Zaragosa houses a daycare center for the children of its students. The alternative school has computers and access to the online Idaho Distance Learning Academy. All teachers and the administrator are White at Zaragosa, whereas almost all of the students are Latino/a.

The graduation rate for Ennis High School is reported as 80% on the district profile. This rate does not include GED or high school equivalency certificates. The State Department of Education reported that Ennis high school has an average dropout rate of 4.78% per year, for an accumulated or cohort rate of 18.8%. Because the data are not disaggregated by ethnicity, it is difficult to ascertain whether a significant number of these dropouts are Latino/a.

Because of low ISAT scores, Ennis High School did not make AYP due to deficiencies in math for Hispanic (HISP) and economically disadvantaged (ECON) students. In response, this district has implemented all-day Limited English Proficiency (LEP) classes to help immigrants and other students with high school academic coursework. Funding for dropout prevention programs is an ongoing issue. Federal funding does not adequately supplement local funding, which, accordiing to the principal, is "insufficient because of the economic downturn in the community." Table 2 provides further details on the rural communities and schools.

CLASSISM AND RACISM IN THREE RURAL COMMUNITIES

Socioeconomic status and racism can create obstacles for rural Latino/a teens that carry enough weight to sink at-risk individuals. School policies and practices can further enhance classism and racism and make school even

TABLE 2. DESCRIPTIONS OF THE RURAL COMMUNITIES AND SCHOOLS

Name of Community	Hagerstown, ID	Juniper Hills, ID	Ennis, ID
General description of community and visual condition	This quiet little town is experiencing a small renaissance, an exception to the rule in rural Idaho. Most homes are older, but well groomed. There seems to be a church on every corner.	This is a low SES area where empty dilapidated buildings dot the main road. There are no grocery stores, just gas stations with convenience stores attached. Schools are in good condition, but there are several barracks that hold classrooms which gives the area a look of impermanence. Property and homes are in poor condition and various stages of decay and neglect are evident. No public transportation is available.	Despite community attempts at revitalization, and pleas to "shop at home," the downtown area barely survives on its small number of shoppers. Population has declined steadily during the last five years, taking with it property values and tax revenues. Empty buildings, once agriculturally based businesses, relay the message that the economic outlook has not improved.
Relationship of Latinos to city government and to school district governance	All authority figures in community/schools are White and most are male. There are no Latino teachers in the high school. The superintendent felt that the dropout issue was very complicated. The city administrator felt that Latinos are marginalized by many and seen as a "problem" that must be tolerated because of the need for farm labor.	All authority figures in the community and schools are White and most are male. There are two Latino/a teachers in the high school. One of the custodians is Latino.	All authority figures in the community and in the schools are White and most are male. The only Latino/a adults in the school are the custodians.
Population size	7,780	3,990	5,645
Percentage of Latino/as in community	29.8%	57%	38.9%

TABLE 2. (*continued*)

Name of Community	Hagerstown, ID	Juniper Hills, ID	Ennis, ID
Median income	$30,074 (below the federal poverty level for a family of eight)	$22,963 (below the federal poverty level for a family of six)	$25, 105 (below the federal poverty level for a family of six) Hispanic Profile data book retrieved 2/4/05 from www2.state.id.us/icha
Economic outlook of community	This community is enjoying better economic prosperity than most in Idaho due to an influx of new industry. It has become a bedroom community to a larger metropolitan area.	Most people who are employed work in the agriculture industry. Seasonal work is common.	Industry closures and a weak farming economy have resulted in reduced school enrollment. The property tax base is low.
Name and description of high school	Hagerstown High School This district was the least accommodating to this study. Several ESL teachers and two vice principals were not familiar enough with students who had recently dropped out to contact them about interviews. The attitude of the educators in this district was that once a student has turned 16 and wants to leave school, there is nothing left to be done.	Juniper Hills High School The person closest to the students was the secretary, a Latina, who was usually surrounded by students between classes. As the students would leave the office, she would call out, "Have a good day, *meja*." (*Meja*, or *mejo* is a term of endearment.) The state website lists a 95% graduation rate, yet a recent class of 40 contained 12 dropouts.	Ennis High School This school was very accommodating to study and was the only one that had a formal dropout prevention plan. The school administrator could not specifically name a Latino/a dropout but mentioned the alternative school as a source.

TABLE 2. (*continued*)

Name of Community	Hagerstown, ID	Juniper Hills, ID	Ennis, ID
Name and description of alternative school	Hagerstown Alternative School Calling this an alternative school is using the term loosely. It has the same basic foundation, but is held at night. The alternative school is more accommodating to regular education students who want to take extra courses in order to free up their days for more electives, or to advance toward an early graduation. None of the participants in the study attended this alternative school due to interference with work schedules. A day school option it would have been better for some participants.	Juniper Hills Alternative School This alternative school is similar to the Zaragosa Alternative School, however the personnel are more rigid and less likely to adapt to at-risk student needs. Students are expelled for violation of attendance policies, even though the facility is out of the town and students are without reliable transportation. Two of the three participants from study tried this alternative school before completing the drop out process. Neither of the two said anything positive about the experience of attending.	Zaragosa Alternative School Participants who attended this school commended the principal and several teachers. School holds two different classes each trimester, and lets out by 1:30 so that students can take PE or other courses at the high school. Transportation is an issue, as it is not provided. No sports, electives, or activities to help students connect with their environment are offered. Day care is available. There are computers and access to the Idaho Distance Learning Academy (IDLA) for students who need to take courses from them. All teachers and administrators are White and there are no Latino/a educators.
Ways in which districts works to include Latinos and other minorities	This school has no formal plans.	This school tracks students through the attendance office and notifies parents when students are absent. Additional Title I classes in grades 9–12 are geared toward reducing the dropout rate.	This school has no formal plans.
Percentage of Latino/as enrolled in school.	25%	58%	40%

TABLE 2. (*continued*)

Name of Community	Hagerstown, ID	Juniper Hills, ID	Ennis, ID
Percentage of adults aged 25 and older who have graduated from high school	71.8% (factfinder.census.gov)	46.4%	65.3%
Percentage of recent high school completion.	68%	71%	80%
Statements about districts made by teachers, administrators, and community members	According to a probation officer, the problem is not with students choosing to drop out, but with the district's zero-tolerance policy that is being used to expel students who fight or use weapons or drugs. Alternative school is a night school, which seems to be only the next step on the way to dropping out. Alternative school does not offer child care, and has no transportation. Fewer classes are offered, and there is no counseling for troubled youth. Night classes are often used by regular education students to help them graduate sooner or make room for electives. Students can take advantage of the HEP program (High School Equivalency), but many students who qualify are reluctant to leave their communities to study in the state capital.	Principal said that ELL students are said to be "the ones most likely to drop out because they cannot pass the 10th grade ISAT." A teacher said that the principal was suggesting that maybe they shouldn't work so hard to keep these kids in school because when they stayed their ISAT scores put the school in failure status: "Maybe we should just let them go if they want to go." Another district employee stated that "these kids do not see dropping out as a bad thing." The principal noted that student athletes undergo grade checks every three weeks. If the student is failing any class they become ineligible to play until the next three week's check. Often students are ineligible for most of the season.	According to a probation officer, there is strong support by juvenile justice to keep kids in school. Kids who are removed because of the zero-tolerance law are required to either attend alternative school or work on the GED through the community college. This officer mentioned that the high school pushes out kids who are academically challenged, but works to keep troubled kids who score well on the ISATS. The school calls and makes sure the high-scoring kids will be in school for the ISAT testing days.
Percentage of free/reduced meals in school district	39%	67%	52%

TABLE 2. (*continued*)

Name of Community	Hagerstown, ID	Juniper Hills, ID	Ennis, ID
Status of NCLB in the high schools for the 2003–4 school year	Hagerstown High School did not make AYP because of Hispanic reading proficiency (www.sde.state.id.us)	Juniper Hills High School did not make AYP because of reading and math proficiency for economic disadvantaged population.	Ennis High School did not make AYP because of math proficiency in the Hispanic and economic disadvantage subgroups.
Status of dropout prevention or reentry programs and interventions.	Elementary and secondary summer school sessions have been scheduled for identified at-risk students. School supports La Raza, an active Youth Leadership program, and has initiated a Latino school newspaper. The student body president is Latina. (Personal communication with high school vice principal).	This year, a dropout prevention program has been implemented which includes a mentoring program. Volunteers are scarce and there is a high staff and administrative turnover, and unstable community ties. The high school relies on teachers to take an individual interest in students. Increased funding is needed for after-school tutoring programs, as well as for an additional part-time staff person to coordinate volunteers.	All-day ESL classes are held. The district is considering an alternative assessment, which includes several measures, to be used for students who are unable to pass the 10th-grade ISAT. The proposed intervention program includes career academies, peer tutors, a Newcomers center (English language immersion), access to distance learning, and after-school English and math labs. Students will be assigned a grade-level teacher to stay with them throughout their high school careers. Parents will be notified when students have two or more zeroes in a class. However, the school is out of the town and no transportation is provided.

more difficult for struggling students. For example, Latino/a students chose friends who were similarly on tight budgets to deal with issues such as lunch. An open campus arrangement was common in these rural schools, and students who could afford it often drove to town to grab a quick lunch during the half hour break. Lacking either transportation, the money to buy lunch in town, or both, Latino/a students often went without lunch rather than eat in the school cafeteria, which was viewed as socially unacceptable. The open campus arrangement thus exacerbated the gap between "rich" and "poor."

Latino/a student athletes seemed to navigate the murky waters of social acceptability a little easier than the non-athletes because they were accorded high status for their athletic abilities. But they also faced economic obstacles, such as needing a lunch to take on the bus to away games and appropriate equipment not provided by athletic funds. For these rural schools, one of the repercussions of the No Child Left Behind Act was that athletic fees were passed on to participants. There was less stigma attached to athletic ineligibility due to obtaining poor grades or "lacking interest" than to admitting that the cost of team shoes, athletic gear, or pay-to-play fees were too high. Simple changes in policies, or actively seeking sponsorship for athletics and academics, could have made a world of difference in the lives of these students.

Another issue for the Latino/a students in these rural schools was transportation to and from school. When community leaders decided to build a new high school on the outskirts of town, students who could not drive had to ride the school bus, also known to the students as the "loser cruiser." High school parking lots, as in most U.S. high schools, were filled with cars, a visual testament that riding the school bus was social suicide. It was more acceptable in the rural high school student culture to walk or drive an older, often unreliable, vehicle that could break down at any moment than to ride the bus to school.

The front yards of many dilapidated homes in these rural communities were graveyards for at least two cars, used to piece together a functional third. "My car broke down," was a mantra to excuse absences, even when untrue. It was better to say the car broke down than to admit that neither of the student's school shirts were clean. For many rural Latino/a high school students, life was spent avoiding the appearance of poverty. Even the ubiquitous high school yearbook became an obstacle for the poor. Very few could afford the yearbook, considered an optional luxury at a cost of between $30 and $50 dollars. Luckily the school libraries kept several copies or many of the students would never have seen them; unfortunately, they were one of the first items that "disappeared" from the library shelves.

A number of Latino/a students left school when employment in rural farm labor was nonexistent in the winter months and traveled to Mexico with their families. Students from Ennis High School had access to the Idaho Distance Learning Academy (IDLA), which provided high school credit for courses completed online. However, that opportunity rested on the assumption that students would have access to a computer and the Internet during their stay in Mexico. Of the nine participants in this study, only one had computer access in their homes in the United States, let alone while traveling to visit relatives in Mexico.

Finally, the rural schools and communities described in this chapter seemed to accept the Latino/a dropout rate. For instance, educators in Hagerstown stated that once a student turns 16 and wants to leave school there is nothing left to be done. A city administrator lamented that Latino/as were seen as a problem that must be tolerated because of the need for farm labor. Social class definitely had an influence on whether or not students were able to find success in public school, and social class analysis is crucial, given the growing divisions of wealth and power in America. Noguera (2003) found in his study that students from low-income families were often treated by schools as a captured audience. He used the example of the school secretary in a poor inner-city school who had a sign on her desk, "This is not Burger King. You can't have it your way!" (p. 83). In contrast, higher socioeconomic groups were treated with respect. Educators knew that parents who were the civic elite had the political clout to demand more, and if they did not receive services in public schools they would likely send their children to private schools.

Latino/a youths in our rural study were captive to the system in a similar way to the students in the Noguera study (2003) and could not "have it their way." There were some accommodations made to Latina/o students, such as the student club La Raza in one school. However, the students who dropped out did not participate in school events in high school. They felt invisible, unimportant, feared or disliked by educators, as revealed in the following case studies. There may be a temptation to blame the students as "naughty kids" but that was not the case. These youths were and are bright, capable, and caring. Only one of the students, Maria, took special education classes and with more attention paid to her IEP (Individualized Education Plan) even Maria could have succeeded. Had these youths had a supportive environment in school, with mentors who valued who they are and held expectations for their success, their lives would have been quite different.

CHAPTER FOUR

Case Studies

LATINA YOUTH EXPERIENCES IN AND OUT OF SCHOOL

SILVIA

"People at school didn't want me to succeed . . . Sometimes the teacher won't even bother with you because you are Hispanic."

Silvia described herself as outspoken and hyper. A typical day for her was spent listening to music, getting ready for the day, and working at one of the three part-time jobs she had taken on since leaving high school last year. She promised her parents, whom she still lived with, that she would complete the GED, but had not yet achieved that goal. Silvia had several friends still in school, and often met with them in the evenings to watch movies or just hang out. She did not plan to stay out of school for much longer, but admitted that at age 16 she is not ready for higher education. "But, just because I dropped out doesn't mean I don't want to continue. I don't want to be flipping burgers, you know. I want to do something." She liked sports, working on cars, shopping, and boys.

Silvia dropped out of high school at the age of 15. She had completed ninth grade, and was midway through her sophomore year. Silvia's grades were above average throughout elementary and junior high school, but plummeted in ninth grade. In seventh grade, Silvia was diagnosed with a physical disability that would progressively worsen and eventually be debilitating. It was difficult to detect the problem so far, and a casual observer would assume that Silvia was healthy.

Although Silvia had an Individualized Education Plan (IEP), once she entered eighth grade she felt it was difficult to get IEP accommodations from the teaching staff. Public schools are required to develop an IEP for every student with a disability who is found to meet federal and state requirements for special education. This persisted even after meetings initiated by Silvia's parents, who were educated professionals and thus different from the other eight students in this study, whose families were employed in farm labor. Silvia objected that she was overlooked in school, and she did not respond well to the negative attention she was given when she requested the accommodations. According to her parents, Sylvia developed oppositional attitudes toward school and teachers for the first time. She received no counseling services through the school although she began to accumulate a disciplinary record. Most offenses were for tardiness and minor fights with other female students.

At the beginning of her ninth-grade school year, Silvia moved in with her grandparents and attended school in an even smaller school district. She reported enjoying the high school there and the close relationships between students and teachers. "I think the class sizes had a big difference in the way the teachers were, because they were able to have a one-to-one relationship with students in each class; they had the time to do that," she said during one of the interviews. She was involved in all aspects of school life. "I just had things going on all the time with being involved in school, school activities, basketball games, and basketball practices."

However, Silvia missed her family, because she could only see them for one or two days a month, and at the end of the first semester she returned home. She enrolled in a charter school for the second semester, but disliked the high-level of independent learning and lack of peer interaction. By the end of that summer, Silvia felt she was ready to try Hagerstown High School. She enrolled for the 10th-grade year, but quickly found the atmosphere stressful. There were a lot of classes to attend, and once again there were teachers who were not willing to make accommodations.

Silvia was familiar with the tests of the No Child Left Behind Act (2002), and felt she would have passed the spring semester's 10th-grade Idaho Standards Achievement Tests (ISAT) had she not left school. She did not mind being tested, but confided that she thought she would rather "show" teachers what she knew. "Why can't we write what we know or make a presentation? That would show more than a test, or more than an A, B, or C answer. I am one of those kids that doesn't test well. I mean, I wish I could break that. But it goes way back. Breaking that freeze-frame that you have when you test because you feel like you won't do well, that's hard."

At the high school, Silvia was not focused on academics as much as she was on relationships. She did not really belong to any of the cliques that existed and was often the target for harassment. She described high school as "basically like living in the real world. What I mean is that you are judged by things such as clothes or race. You have the high class and the low class, and a lot of teachers and administrators will work with the kids that help the school reputation, like in athletics or academic-wise. But the lesser kids— the kids who aren't really involved with the school but want to do well in school—aren't really encouraged . . . I was definitely low on the food chain."

Silvia perceived that teachers showed favoritism toward high-status students, White students, and students whose parents were financially well-off. She became outspoken about these opinions and was kicked out of class by several teachers for her remarks. Silvia believed that schools did not really care about kids, and that they were more concerned with grades and school image. The school's "actions don't show that they actually care about the students. And you can read that. Any kid in high school can read in between those lines."

Although being involved in sports was very important to Silvia, she did not find success on the basketball court in high school like she had in her previous school. The team had been playing together for a while and was not willing to be inclusive. She had worked out all summer hoping to be able to play high school basketball. However, after complaining to the coach about the way some of the girls were treating others, she noticed that she was playing less and sitting on the bench more. Silvia was getting roughed up on the basketball court during practice, and after being called "spic" one day she just gave up trying, took off her jersey, and walked out. No one invited her back, and she did not return to the court. Silvia loved to play basketball, but "they made it so I wouldn't even want to play for that school anymore. That's how my feelings are towards them."

In the classroom, Silvia was struggling as well. She felt she was not learning anything, and if she was working on something that she did not understand the teachers would not provide help. "I would say, 'OK. I don't get this.' And it would turn into an argument because the teacher would make me feel like I was dumb if I didn't get it. If you don't get something the first time they explain it, they aren't going to go through it again." Silvia would argue with teachers and end up being assigned to detention. "My grades dropped drastically. My grades went downhill because there was no point in asking questions if you're going to get kicked out of class for doing it."

Silvia thought that the educators showed racist attitudes in dealing with Latino/a students. "If they could single you out in class they would. If you caused a little tiny problem, they'd blow it way out of proportion and make it a huge deal—more than it ever should have been. Like for instance, there was a fight between a White kid and a Hispanic. The White kid started the fight, but the Hispanic was the one who got expelled from school. The White kid got suspended for a day. That's how it is."

Silvia was critical of teaching practices that required students to do what she called "busy work." "They teach a 20- or 30-minute lesson—some of them don't even do that—hand out worksheets, and then grade them when we're done. They sit at their desks and you hand it in; you do the same thing over and over. That's their lesson plan." She mentioned repeatedly that it was important to her to feel like she was learning something, but most of her experiences at Hagerstown High School were not learning experiences. "If you're not learning anything, I don't see the point of high school," she remarked. "I didn't learn anything. I know as much now as I did in 8th grade."

When asked about positive experiences or teachers in this school district, Silvia could not think of any. "There were very few teachers from kindergarten on that were behind me. I think, without counting the other school I went to when I lived with my grandparents, I only had three who cared about me. I mean, those three actually let me know. There's something off about that, only having three. If you can go to your next class and not have to deal with the hallway bull crap. If you go in and feel safe and secure because you have that one-on-one relationship with the teacher, then that's enough to keep you going through school. But if you have to worry about the same thing in class that you worry about in the hall and bathrooms, then, no way."

The best teacher Silvia had in Hagerstown was a physical education teacher at the high school. Silvia recounted how this teacher connected with youths and made them feel important. "My brother had him too, and he'll drive all the way back home just to see that teacher and spend time with his family. My brother's friends do that, too. I think that's really awesome."

A huge issue for Silvia was peer relationships. She mentioned harassment by other girls as one of her main concerns. Starting with junior high, there had been problems with other girls writing threatening notes, calling names, and damaging Silvia's school locker and personal items. She was often involved in battles over boyfriends, and needed to switch classes to get away from certain factions of the student body. "Some of the things they [other girls] did were not at school. They went after my little sister and stalked her, scared her. They slashed the tires on our car, threw a rock through the house window, stole my stuff and spread it all over the school. They'd put notes in my locker with words like 'slut' or words in that category. It was just so bad and I could take the notes to the principal and he really didn't do anything about it."

Silvia's parents, who were professionals, arranged for her to attend weekly sessions with a private counselor to deal with to Silvia's anxiety. "I was so frustrated that I didn't have any more energy to keep doing the same thing over and over again or keep fighting back." Worried, Silvia's parents agreed to put her on antidepressants to hopefully help her get through these tumultuous times. She had been caught smoking, and was on probation for driving without privileges. Her parents had worked hard to elevate themselves, through education, into a middle-class lifestyle. College graduates, they both felt stymied by school administrators who had failed their expectations to help Silvia feel safe and wanted at school. They were aware of Silvia's strong personality and frequent problems with peers, but were not able to steer the course of Silvia's high school career in a different direction (personal communication with Silvia's mother).

Two days before Silvia dropped out she was in the principal's office with her parents. There had been another incident with harassment, and a fight with a group of girls had occurred. According to Silvia, it was the principal who suggested that maybe there were options, other than regular high school, that Silvia and her parents should consider. "My thoughts were, 'What the hell?' I mean, this is the principal, and I didn't expect him to be suggesting dropping out. It kind of took me by surprise," Silvia said. The principal and Silvia's parents talked about the GED (General Education Diploma) and the HEP (High School Equivalency Program). Her parents did not want her to go to an alternative school because they believed it was for "bad kids." No decision was made at that time, but Silvia felt that the principal wanted her out of the school and off of his work load.

Two days later, several girls accosted her verbally during a class that was being supervised by a substitute teacher. Normally the teacher in the class was able to keep these incidents from happening, but the substitute teacher was not. When Silvia walked out of the class, she could hear the girls calling her a slut. The substitute teacher did not get involved. "I just couldn't take it anymore," Silvia confided. She went to the office to check out of school, but the principal did not come out of his office. A secretary took the paperwork in to him, and he signed it and sent it back. "I think that there was a problem that he thought just couldn't happen in his school. And if the problem went away—which was me—then everything would go back to normal."

Silvia's mother picked her up and took her home, where she ate lunch, took a shower and crawled into bed. "I didn't know what else to do. What to think. I just needed a couple of days, I thought, to gather myself. My parents . . . they were, like, well . . . go to church and re-find yourself. I just needed some time to emotionally and physically pull myself together. For my parents the place to do that is church, but two of the girls [who were harassing her] went to my church, so it wasn't a comforting place for me like it was for my parents."

In the beginning, Silvia recalled being frustrated and sad, but soon feelings of relief that she didn't have to go back prevailed. When she was little she had wanted to grow up to be an airplane pilot. Today she just wants to make enough money to be able to do things with her friends. When asked how other people view dropouts, she replied, "They think that you were too lazy to do the work. They don't think you are worth very much if you drop out. If you go for a job and say that you have dropped out, they're not going to look at you very hard." She felt that some kids drop out because of a lack of communication between them and school employees, and that some kids feel like teachers don't want to deal with them if they have problems.

As Silvia had already found, it was difficult for her to be a Latina athlete in her rural, Idaho school. "Playing sports and being Hispanic is definitely hard in this community because you also aren't LDS [Latter Day Saint], and that plays a big part in this community, what your religion is. Hispanics don't get to be involved in basketball; you don't see very many. Mostly just in soccer. The basketball coach doesn't have high expectations for us, and even the other coaches don't put much into us." She worried that the White leaders in the community did not expect much from Latino/as and had stereotyped impressions of them as troublemakers, thought they were involved in gangs, and considered them as probable high school dropouts.

One of the most difficult times for Silvia was right before school started the fall after she had dropped out. Her sister and friends were excitedly shopping, and she went along with them but regretted it. "I saw one of my old teachers at the store. She didn't even acknowledge that I was there, but it isn't like it hurt my feelings or anything. I didn't want to talk to her." Running into former classmates was also difficult for Silvia. She wondered if she had made the right decision in dropping out. "Everyone was so excited to go back to school so that they could see everyone. I missed seeing a lot of people, but I don't think going back would be worth it. I love my friends, but I shouldn't have to go back to that just to see my friends for an extra eight hours of school. Especially when all everyone does is gossip to make people's lives miserable."

When asked how she would describe what dropping out is like, she said, "People at school just didn't want me to succeed, so I always felt angry about it. For me, nobody was going to admit that there were hazing or harassment problems in the school." Silvia had suggestions for how the school could have been more supportive. "I think if I would have had more teacher support I would still be there. If you can go in class and feel safe and secure because you have a one-on-one relationship with the teacher, that's probably enough to keep you going through school. But there are a lot of things going on that people don't even realize; it's easier for them to ignore it. It's almost like that movie, *The Matrix*. There's only what you look at. And you think it's real because that's what they give you to look at. So, your principal gives you the image of what your school is, because that's what he wants you to see. If he sees the flaws, everyone sees the flaws. He doesn't want them to see, so he doesn't admit it."

When asked what she would do differently, Silvia couldn't think of anything that she had the power to change. "If I had stayed just to finish high school, my personality, who I was, would have just deteriorated because I would have had to keep my mouth shut. I would have had to have been a lower person, and that's not who I am." Silvia felt that she was a stronger person for standing up for herself, even when she felt alone doing it. Being Latina, in her view, meant fighting against a negative identity given by society. She talked about Latino/a friends who had self-image problems, who did not think they were worth very much, and who would just try to get by. "But not me, I refuse to be part of it. For me, dropping out wasn't failing, it was succeeding."

CRISTINA

"I would take my work home and do it. I would never do it in school."

Cristina's typical day after dropping out of school went like this: "I clean house and just go out and look for jobs. And I also go help my grandma. She needs help around the house and so I go help her and that's about it." She said her day did not really start until her boyfriend, a high school dropout as well, got home from work. Then they would "hang out, watch movies, or go with friends, that kind of thing." Cristina dropped out of high school when she was 17. She had never attended the regular high school in Ennis, but had moved directly from junior high school to Zaragosa Alternative High School. "All my friends were over there, and I heard that it was a good school because they help you a lot better and everything."

At the time of the interviews, Cristina was 18. She had spent 11 years in school, but had not accumulated enough credits to be considered a junior. Her grades had been mostly Ds and Fs since middle school. "Since I've been at the alternative school I've met a whole bunch of people who went to regular high school, and they couldn't catch up with their work. They just stay at alternative [high school] because they get through more classes. Some people go back and forth, but when they do go back over there [regular high school], pretty soon they come back because you only have two classes and you don't have to worry about all that work."

Cristina was chronically absent from school. She lived a couple of miles from the school, but did not always have transportation. The alternative school did not provide transportation, so this was an ongoing issue for

Cristina. She missed a lot of school, and when she did go to school, she could never manage to get there on time. "Mainly I was absent because I didn't have a ride into town. With tardies, I wouldn't wake up in time or I didn't like the way my hair looked or something like that. That's about it when I was absent, except for the times when I went to jail."

Other problems, according to her teachers, included lack of completion of assignments, not paying attention in class, a "defiant attitude" toward a male teacher, and an overall "negative attitude" toward academics. "I was the student who liked math and probably biology. Those were really fun classes. I was a troublemaker. I wouldn't listen to the teachers, and I would do my own thing. I would take my work and do it at home. I would never do it at school, and that was a problem. I wanted to talk and visit and write letters. I was a talkative person, and I got in a lot of trouble in junior high, too."

She needed seven more classes to graduate, but also had 20 credits that were listed as "incomplete" on her transcript. Cristina arrived at the alternative school relatively low in math and English skills. Her reading was at an 8th-grade level, and she had not passed ISAT testing, although she had made several attempts. One teacher described Cristina as being "test phobic," but Cristina claimed that tests made her only a little nervous, "but not that much."

Cristina expressed a concern for students who were English language learners (ELL) or had Limited English Proficiency (LEP) status because she felt they were targets of discrimination from other students and teachers. "Some say that if they can't speak English they shouldn't be in school. I think that is rude, but there are some other Mexicans here who can speak English that will help them."

She was vague about her academic progress and did not seem to know her grade point average or the number of credits she had acquired. Cristina's account of her academic career differed from the comments of her teachers. "She's smoked herself stupid," one teacher remarked. Cristina's main problem was drug addiction, specifically methamphetamines. "Last year I went to drug court, and I just barely graduated from there in August. They encourage you to come to school and get it done, but it doesn't mean you have to do the work. You just have to have a C to make them satisfied."

Overall, Cristina spoke little about the academic side of schooling and focused on relationships with peers. She could not name a memorable learning experience. In fact, the reason she decided to attend alternative school instead of trying regular high school was because many of her friends were at the alternative school. Cristina admitted, "I didn't really have problems; I just wanted to be in school because my friends were there."

One teacher remarked that Cristina was "sexually active" at a young age and often made "sexually explicit, inappropriate remarks" in class. Cristina was said to "stir things up" with other students, and there were reports of defiance and opposition to educators. This teacher believed that part of this was an effort to gain attention, and part of it was a diversionary tactic to detract from her inability to perform at a high school academic level.

Cristina was never involved in sports, cheerleading, or student clubs. Going directly from junior high to the alternative school and never attending regular high school did not help because the alternative school did not provide extracurricular programs. Even a student who needed a PE course, a requirement for graduation, would have to reconnect with the regular high school because there were not facilities or instructors for that in the alternative setting. The same was true for courses such as American government, advanced technology, and driver's education. "They don't have driver's education in this school, so you have to go to the high school to get it. If you do that, then you're late for morning classes [at the alternative high school] and you have to make up the classes or you won't get your credit. I think that's kind of stupid. If you are taking driver's ed, then you should be able to take it and not have to make up the classes you miss [at the alternative high school]."

Cristina cited only a few teachers and one administrator as caring about her during her entire school career. She described the Zaragosa alternative high school principal as "a caring person who would always be there for anybody who had problems or anything. He talks to them [students] and gets to know them." Notably, this principal made the effort to call students on the telephone, and encourage them to re-enroll when they quit, and to not give up. "He's been calling me and telling me to come back. He tells me, 'You need to get those credits. You can do it. You'll get that diploma.'" The best teacher she ever had "was Mrs. G. because she'll help you understand what she is talking about. When she read a story she'd involve you in it. She used different voices and everything to make you really interested." The worst teacher was Mr. J. because "he would just tell you to do the work and wouldn't help you with it."

Most of Cristina's comments about school revolved around interactions, positive and negative, with her peer group. School was about friends and the activities they were involved in together. She claimed no gang involvement; however, she had a tattoo on her hand that was a well-known symbol for one of the local gangs. One of the negatives about school, according to Cristina, was fighting and people getting mad at each other. "Last year there were a lot of fights around gangs. That's the main thing here, the gangs. I'm not into that stuff."

Since leaving school, she did not miss the fighting and gossip, but she did miss talking to her friends. "I got in fights with a lot of girls, and I argued with them and called them names. I had to go to the cop's office (that was in junior high), and I didn't get along with very many people. The arguments were always about stupid little things that I don't even remember. Probably some girl said something about me."

Cristina said dropping out of school in this small, rural community was common. "I don't think most people are even bothered by people who drop out because there are a lot of kids who drop out around here. I know about 30 kids who have dropped out of school. That's a lot of people." But she saw disadvantages to not being in school. "I think school is a lot better because it keeps me out of trouble. There is more stuff to do in school, and you can wake up and go to school."

Cristina's mom graduated from high school, but her father did not. Cristina's parents were divorced and her dad lived in another town. She saw him infrequently. Until this year, Cristina lived with her mother and grandmother. She had an older brother who also dropped out, but did not live at home. At the end of her 10th-grade year, Cristina moved out of state to pursue seasonal farm labor employment with her mother. When she returned in late September, it was too late to enroll for the trimester. Cristina did not go back to school, and "Mom didn't say anything except 'If you want to go back that's a good idea because you don't have that many credits left to go, but if you don't want to go back you can always find a job.' The school people [teachers and staff] didn't say anything about me dropping out."

Cristina described her dad as not being around very much. "My mother helped me with my work and let me read to her and stuff like that. She was a really good person to help with school work." Over the years, both parents and an uncle encouraged Cristina to stay in school, and she believed that "you can't get a good job without an education, without a diploma anyway." Cristina had little experience with the job market, and did not consider the implications of not having a diploma when actually trying to get a job. "I've just applied in grocery stores, and I tried to get a job at gas stations. But you can't work there until you're 19 because they sell beer."

Cristina said she would like to become a beautician, but she had no formal plan for achieving that goal, believing it would happen sometime in the future. "Cutting hair is one thing I like to do, and doing nails. I don't know what else really. I want to do regular stuff, get married, and have kids. In five years I probably see myself getting a college education because I really want to go to beauty college. I'll encourage my kids to stay in school, and help them with their work. Tell then that I dropped out, and encourage them to stay in school."

At the time of the interviews, Cristina lived with her boyfriend and his parents, but did not yet contribute financially to the arrangement. She was looking for work and finding work difficult to find. She had a police record for driving without privileges and drug possession; she was on probation.

One condition of her probation was that she either work toward graduation or get the GED. However, once she turned 18 those expectations disappeared, and at 17, Cristina no longer felt the need to stay in school, especially because most of her friends had either finished or dropped out.

"A dropout is a person that didn't like school and didn't want to go. I don't think that most people are even bothered by people dropping out, but . . . I would tell other kids to just go to school. Have fun while you are there and get along with everybody. I'd tell them to get involved with activities. And that getting to know other people is about the coolest thing I've done at school."

MARIA

"They [teachers] always go to another person and they never came over to see if I need help. It's been like that for a long time, since before I started high school."

In the dark street outside the apartment, a small group of kids played, but it was mostly quiet in the old neighborhood. At the second knock, the door opened into the family room, which also served as the dining room. The family was waiting for this interview, and sitting around a large wooden table that took up most of the room. Mexican music was playing low in the background. A parakeet chirped in the cage hanging in the doorway of the kitchen. An orange, striped kitten weaved back and forth through the legs of the dining room chairs. Every available shelf space held knickknacks. The white and gray stained walls were covered with religious depictions of the Madonna and Jesus. The five-room apartment was clean and tidy, but full.

This was the home of Maria, a slightly chubby 16-year-old. Her dark eyes sparkled. During the interview, on an evening after she had returned home from work, her mouth often twisted in a self-conscious way as she searched for the right words to explain her experience. Maria began her academic career in Juniper Hills at the age of four by attending Head Start, and ended it by dropping out of Juniper Hills High School at the beginning of 11th grade. She had just turned 16.

Maria had been labeled by school personnel as a special education student and has had an Individualized Education Plan (IEP) since elementary school. According to the resource room teacher, Maria was "holding her own in resource and mainstreamed classes until ISAT testing was initiated in 2001." But, according to Maria, the problem started before that. In high school, Maria frequently complained to her parents that she did not get help from the teachers, and that the school work was hard. "They [teachers] always go to another person and they never came over to see if I need help. It's been like that for a long time, since before I started high school."

Maria was also labeled as Limited English Proficiency (LEP). In elementary school she thrived under the protection of one classroom teacher each year, but as she moved up through the middle school and into high school, the number of teachers and classes was overwhelming. Even special education classes didn't alleviate the stress. "Math, I hated math and science. I never liked those classes, but I liked reading and writing. I hated history too. Then they changed the history and I didn't understand it that much either. Every year you would have new teachers and new subjects. The classes were so hard. They said I would like music appreciation, or something like that, and it was hard. I didn't understand nothing about it. The teachers go to help another person. They just say, 'Wait, I need to help this other person.' And I waited and they never helped me."

When it was time for 10th-grade ISAT testing, Maria remembered being nervous, but "I went upper on it. I didn't know how because I was just (mimes picking at the keyboard)." She laughed about it. "I don't know how I did. If they wanted that we should know the questions, they should give you more practice." Taking the 10th-grade ISAT was a little easier, in Maria's opinion, than the previous year because she could get help by having someone read items to her. "I did understand that better, but another year I didn't understand it and I done really bad."

The ISAT tests need to be easier to understand, in Maria's opinion. "Because people like me don't understand big words. They just want us to do the tests, and we don't understand. We aren't going to learn if we don't get all the big words. I like to get good grades, and I didn't like it when I didn't. It made me not want to do it anymore, and it felt bad."

Maria mentioned that her second-grade teacher was the best teacher she ever had. "Mrs. T. was nice because she helped us and she never said wait for another person. And then in middle school Mr. S. was good because he helped us learn good, and with him I didn't have to change class." Maria couldn't think of anything else positive about middle school except for being in the band in 7th grade, even though she had to quit because her father wouldn't allow her to attend evening events at the school.

Two particular teachers in high school were mentioned as being the worst because they gave tests and didn't help her learn what she needed to do well on the tests. "One teacher would take us to her class. When we had a test, they would always take us to her class and study there. She let us look at our notes, and then put them away. And then we were supposed to remember what was on them. Sometimes I never remembered nothing."

Maria alluded to racism in the school as an issue, noticing attitudes among older people in the community and some teachers. "They never say nothing, but I think sometimes they don't like us. Like they're better than us. And I don't like that. But some Whites aren't like that with Spanish people. Some people do care."

Maria complained about teasing from classmates. Other girls would tease her and tell her she looked pregnant. Maria thought the harassment was because they thought she was a bad girl. She explained that she could not be a bad girl because of how strict her parents were. "My dad never let us go out. My parents always take good care of us, so I don't know why they are saying that."

Maria still had a few close friends at the high school and missed seeing them regularly. She did not see her friends that often anymore unless she happened to run into them walking around or at the stores. She spent most of her free time with her family. As graduation approached, she felt badly that she would not be among her friends, but added, "I'm glad I got a job [working with her mother in the onion sheds and with the cherries during cherry season] and went on with that."

Neither of Maria's parents spoke English well, and the two daughters who live at home usually spoke both English and Spanish for their parents. Maria's older sister, who had just turned 18, was also in special education classes. She hoped to graduate but was worried about passing the state testing requirement. These were the two youngest children, and the last ones at home. Maria had seven older bothers and sisters. Only one brother had graduated.

Maria said that most of the children in the family had dropped out at 16 because school was too hard for them. Maria's parents encouraged all their children to finish high school. "But I didn't. They say that it is up to me, and that in school I have a better chance for work than if I don't go to school. They always told me that, but I never listened."

Maria claimed that she actually started thinking about dropping out when she was in 9th grade. That summer while working she remembered thinking that she would like to work in a store or clean for people instead of being in school. Gradually, throughout 10th-grade the thought grew. By the time she turned 16, a few months into 11th grade, she did not talk to anyone about leaving school; she just quit going. "I was thinking about it and thinking about it. So I did it. My mom and dad didn't want me to, but then I got a call to go to work and they needed me, and so I did that."

Maria's mother called the school and informed them that Maria was dropping out. "The secretary asked why and everything, and one other teacher called and told me to think about it, but I said, 'No, I already thought about it and I want to drop out of school.'" Maria seemed content to work and enjoyed being with her family. Some months after dropping out she ran into a former teacher in the grocery store. "One of the teachers said they'd never seen me happy at school, so they know. She said if I was happy dropping out of school, then that was good."

Maria felt she was much happier working. "I get off of work and take a shower and then I watch TV. I go to work at eight in the morning. At work I take out the rotten onions and the light ones and the colored ones. They don't want the white or purple onion[s]. In summer I work in the cherries. I like my jobs. Sometimes I help out the family with money, and sometimes the rest of it is mine."

Maria has heard about getting a GED. Although she wasn't sure at the time what it meant, she thought if the classes were held at night and she could still go to work she might be interested. As a child she wanted to be a teacher, and she thinks maybe after a while she will think about that some more. For now, Maria would like to work and then get married and be a mom. "My dad wants me to wait until I'm like 25 to get married!" She thought that was a horrible idea, but admitted her dad might not let her date until then. As the youngest child of a large family she was watched over by many caring family members.

Maria had been taught to believe that education is important, but also believed, "You could find a good job not going to school." If someone told her they were thinking of dropping out, she would tell them that if they want to do it, they should. She was the student who "didn't care about school. My teachers would say I was a good student, but sometimes I talked back to them because I didn't want to do the work because it was hard. Maybe people think that I was a bad girl to drop out. If I was a boy they would think I was in trouble or something. It seems like a bad thing to do, and it makes me feel bad that people think those things." But Maria is not sorry about her decision. To Maria, dropping out was better because the school work was too difficult. "Dropping out means it made my life easier by not having homework and not staying up until 12 at night doing homework."

BEATRIZ

"I was on the dance team in junior high, and I wanted to do it in high school, but I didn't even try out because I knew there was no way I could afford it."

Beatriz dropped out of school at 17. Now, at 19 she had two children and lived with her mother, her brother, and his wife and two children. Beatriz's day revolved around her children and work. She got the children up around 8:30 a.m., and after they were fed, bathed, dressed, and had played for a while, she put them down for naps and got herself ready for the day. Then she cleaned the house and did other chores. Once her children woke up from their morning naps, she played with them, and then got lunch. Her afternoon was spent doing laundry and ironing while the children again napped. She had to be at work at 4:00 p.m., so Beatriz left home as soon as her mother came home from her job to take care of her grandchildren. Beatriz did not own a car, and had to borrow her mother's car or get a ride from a coworker.

Beatriz's mother would tend to the children while Beatriz worked in a restaurant, usually until around 10:00 p.m. On weekends Beatriz worked until midnight, but during the week she came right home from work and put her children to bed before going to bed herself. "And that's about it. The next day I do it all over again. I'm working, and it's a lot, but I'm used to it. On my days off, if I don't have my own kids with me all the time, I have my brother's kids. I always have at least three or four kids with me all the time, no matter what. So, I'm used to it."

Even though Beatriz was pregnant her senior year, she continued to attend school. But after the baby was born, it was difficult for Beatriz to keep up with taking care of her baby and the demands of school. "It was just so hard because of my baby. She was little and it was winter. She would get sick if I took her out. I would miss a day when I took her to the doctor. I didn't have a car, so it was hard to take her to a babysitter and then get to school on time. I couldn't pay a babysitter either because I didn't have a job."

After Beatriz exceeded the absence limit, administrators at Ennis High School suggested that she transfer to the alternative school, which had a daycare. "But it was still hard. I always felt bad dragging her [the baby] out that early in the morning, and it was cold. I was always late, and half the time I never came. And then I just didn't come anymore." So at 17, with just one semester of high school left, Beatriz dropped out.

School had always been enjoyable for Beatriz, and until 9th grade her grades were As and Bs. She had attended schools in Ennis since kindergarten. "I got good grades, I was there every day, and I was always involved. I did all my work. But after my mom and dad got separated, when I was in 8th grade, after that I had trouble." School involvement, especially extracurricular activities, was curtailed after her father moved out. Beatriz's mom was working hard, but there was not enough money for a single parent to provide extras. "I was on the dance team in junior high, and I wanted to do it in high school, but it was too expensive. It was about $2,000 per kid and there were other fees if you had to travel. It was expensive. I didn't even try out because I knew there was no way I could afford it."

At Ennis High School, Beatriz's favorite subjects were history and science. She did poorly in English, and "all right in math, but I was always in the low class, you know, transitions to math or pre-algebra." However she passed all sections of the 10th-grade ISAT tests and, until she had her baby, she was scheduled to graduate on time. "I wasn't scared [of the testing]; I just really didn't want to take the ISATs. They told us, 'This test is very important so you need to pay attention in school so that when the test comes you know everything that's going to be on it.' It was like nothing. I wasn't nervous or anything."

According to Beatriz, the best teachers showed they cared by speaking respectfully to all students, "even Mexicans," and making sure all the kids were getting good grades. She enjoyed teachers that employed cooperative learning methods and group projects. "It would help me to see other ways of doing things. You get more points of view that way." Positive experiences for Beatriz would be when somebody came to her for help, usually in history. "That would be like, 'Wow, they came to me!'" She also recalled two teachers who made her want to be in class. "Everybody got good grades, and everybody wanted to be there. She [the science teacher] made everything fun." The history teacher was mentioned as someone who would always tell her, "Oh, you're such a good kid. If you would just apply yourself you could do so much." To Beatriz, "That was good. It would make me want to work harder, and it was kind of different that someone would say that. I always got along with most of the teachers, but I wasn't the favorite."

The teachers in high school Beatriz did not like were criticized because they did not have an attitude of caring for all students. According to Beatriz, one teacher in particular did not like Mexicans and resented working with them. "Even the kids who weren't Hispanic, kids who were White, would say that she was prejudiced. She would be rude to me, so I would just be rude back to her. I always had an attitude with her, and we never liked each other." Beatriz retaliated by skipping class. This particular teacher taught Fundamentals of Math, a class Beatriz felt the teacher saw as for "dumb kids and Mexicans." Beatriz noted that she was not the only student to dislike the math teacher. "She was the worst teacher I ever had. She was always putting kids down. She would say, 'I already showed you how to do the work. I explained it once, and I'm not going to explain it again.' She was really rude. I mean, she wasn't doing anything except sitting at her desk. She could help us, but she wouldn't. So I just felt like, 'Whatever. I'm not going to do it.' Our class was a bunch of Mexicans, so she hated our class. So, we thought, she's rude so we're going to be rude. She'd say things like, 'Are you guys that dumb that you don't know how to do this?' Or like, everybody would get a bad grade on the test, and she'd say, 'Why do I even waste my time with you guys? You guys don't even try.' I don't know what her trip was. How could she be like that?"

Beatriz had great memories of times at the high school with her friends, and she thought about them often. "It was fun because I was popular and so was my best friend. We were the pretty girls." She also realized she could have had more good times if she had finished her senior year. "Like at assemblies we would all sit together. Those were good times. We would hurry and meet at our lockers between classes and gossip. The beginning of the senior year was fun, but I had to make new friends because my close friends were already graduated and gone, and that was weird."

Beatriz said that while she was in high school she was not aware of any stigma attached to being pregnant in school, and her friends supported her even when she had another child within the next 18 months. "Everybody was really nice about it. They would say, 'Oh, you're getting so fat,' and stuff like that. They would ask if it was going to be a boy or girl, but they didn't look down on me." However, later, after she left school, she felt people looked down on her or were prejudiced. Beatriz also realized that by having children so young, she gave up part of her school experience. "In a way it would have been better to have my kids after I graduated, but that's life. It makes you grow up, so I really grew up quick. It teaches you. I had to get a job and be real responsible. In a way that's good, but in a way I'm not going out with my friends and having fun like I should be. But it doesn't bother me. I'm in my own little world and doing my own thing."

Beatriz had a few problems with harassment by other females in high school which resulted in a fight with one girl. "Well, one time some girl thought I wanted to beat her up and they [school administrators] made a big deal out of it. They said if I looked at her or talked to her I would get kicked out. I didn't even talk to her or care about her. It was her problem, because I didn't do anything to her." Other than that incident, Beatriz had a large group of friends she got along well with. Most of her friends were Latino/a.

After transferring to Ennis Alternative High School, the young mother found it to be a more supportive environment than the regular high school. "I could talk to the principal about getting here on time, and he was really helpful. The other high school teachers didn't care. They would just say, 'Oh, you're late.' They didn't even ask why." Being able to take her baby to school with her was helpful, but Beatriz found that even with a daycare on-site, it was hard to manage school and be a young mother.

The procedures at the alternative school were more flexible, and teachers worked with Beatriz to help her attain enough credits to graduate. However, she quit attending within a few months. "At least he [the alternative school principal] called to see what was going on, and told me that if I decided to come back to call. At the other school I told them I was leaving and they just said, 'OK, just bring all your books back.' They didn't even ask why or anything."

Beatriz attended the ceremony to see her classmates graduate and recalled feeling bad about not finishing. "I went all the way to 12th grade and I didn't even graduate. I felt bad, but then I thought, 'I'll get over it. This isn't the worst thing that could happen.' My sister went with me [to graduation] and she made it into a joke. She said, 'I only made it to 10th grade, don't feel bad.' So we were laughing about it."

The movie, *Remember the Titans*, reminded Beatriz of high school because it was all about friends and the traumas in life that people experience. She recalled with sadness the events surrounding the death of one of her close friends who was in a car accident. "Me and my friends went through some tough times that summer, but then you get older and move on with your life." Beatriz looks forward to attending her class reunion, even though she didn't graduate. "All of my friends and the people who know me know that I'm not the type of person who thinks because I didn't graduate I can't go. I'll go, talk to people, and have fun."

Thinking back to the events that led to dropping out of high school, Beatriz realized that her problems began shortly before she entered ninth grade. Her parents got divorced, and her dad, who had been the disciplinarian in the family, moved out of state. "My dad was really strict on us and we always knew we'd better get As. And when he left us, then me and my brother didn't care about it anymore. We were just really rebellious." Beatriz's mom was hampered in her supervision of Beatriz and her older brother following the divorce because she was working all the time. "She's really to herself, like shy, and doesn't like to talk to people at all." She was able to provide for her two children and encouraged them to stay in school. Beatriz admitted that she got in a lot of trouble at that time. "I got arrested three times. I was in jail for three months each time for drugs, because I got into drugs and stuff like that. My brother did the same stuff, but he never got caught."

Beatriz's mom did not go to school, or contact the teachers. She allowed Beatriz to make her own decisions about staying in school or dropping out. "My dad was gone, and my mom was not really there all the time. She's a real hard worker, and she's not there to see what we do. So we would just not go to school, and she wouldn't know." Beatriz shared that both she and her brother had chronic attendance problems in high school. Mom was never contacted directly about grades or attendance, even though both Beatriz and her brother's attendance issues led to loss of credit and dropping out. Beatriz and her brother were able to intercept the automated phone calls from the school regarding absences, and with their mother at work this was an easy task.

What finally straightened Beatriz out was the knowledge that if she continued to break the law her daughter would be taken from her. "I was going through the process with the law, and it got to a point where I had to take an evaluation. There was a possibility that I would have to go to rehab for a year and I thought, 'No way. I can't leave my daughter.'" At the time of the interviews Beatriz had successfully completed probation, and was confident that her dealings with law enforcement were over. She was told by a probation officer that it would be easier for her to get a GED than to finish high school, even though she only lacked four credits to complete graduation requirements. She was never counseled about the long-term differences in salary, benefits, and results of getting a GED over a regular high school diploma.

Beatriz and her two young children live with her mother. Beatriz's brother, his wife and his children also live with the matriarch. "When I was younger I did really, really good in school and my mom was always happy about that because none of my older brothers and sisters graduated. She always thought I would, so it is kind of hard for her that I didn't finish. She wants me to go to college, and get a better job. It will probably be about a year until I can get on my feet completely to do that. For single parents who are Hispanic and not married there are programs that pay for practically all of your education and college, so I want to do that. I want to get a good job, like an office job, because this waitress stuff doesn't cut it. I know I could do better."

Beatriz's mom dropped out of school in fourth grade to work with her parents in farm labor. Her dad did not graduate, but Beatriz thinks he may have attended some of eighth grade. She was not sure because she could not recall them ever talking about it. "It's kind of hard because we're already thinking, 'Oh, I'm not going to graduate.' That's in our family. Our family didn't graduate. Our moms didn't graduate. Our brothers and sisters didn't graduate, so it's just normal, I guess. When I was little I knew that my mom only made it to the fourth grade because she had to work. My brothers and sisters were always in trouble with the law. My family has a past of being in trouble all the time. I guess when we were little we just saw that and so we tend to do the same things."

Beatriz was not afraid of working, and remained dedicated to taking good care of her two children. She wanted to eventually have her own house, and planned to marry her children's father. When she was younger, she wanted to be a lawyer. "But a lawyer is out of the question now because you have to go to college for so long. That would be kind of hard. I still think about being a cop, but that's not the main thing I want to do. I want to have a good job, like an office job. I don't want to be nothing big. I just like being simple. Being a mom is enough." She did not want to continue working in a restaurant forever, but Beatriz also feared losing that job because work was scarce in Ennis. Luckily, "even in hard times people like to go out to eat."

According to Beatriz, having children was the best thing that ever happened to her. "They have everything they need. That's something to be proud of, I think. They are real happy kids." She does not regret having them, even if she did have to give up high school and fun with friends. "It's kind of hard because people are prejudiced against you, or they look down on you. Like now I have two kids. I do really good with my kids, but people say things to me like, 'Oh, you're 18 with two kids?' And I think, 'What do they care? What's it to them'?"

Beatriz found that defining the word "dropout" was difficult. At one time she would have thought it was a person who was in trouble, or was a bad kid. "That usually is the case, but you shouldn't look at it like that. Everybody has their own reasons for doing things. I tell myself that I had a really hard time because I had a kid. I had something going and then gave up on it. I gave up on school. Now, even if I don't want to do something I'm still going to try hard if it's going to be good for me and my kids. Dropping out is hard. People should explain to kids and talk to them about how they are going to feel later on down the road. That gets to people. It really got to me when I went to my graduation, and I didn't graduate. You need to sit down and talk to kids individually, not as a group, about problems and see if there is a way to help each kid. If I could talk to kids I would tell them to be really involved in school activities. That's probably why I got pregnant because I didn't get involved that much. Just don't get a boyfriend," she laughed.

SOPHIA

"The [good] teacher, the fun way she did it was different. . . . The other teachers say, 'Here's the book. Do whatever you want.'"

"In the morning I get up, and take a shower. I take the baby, Daniel, into the shower with me. We get ready and Daniel goes to daycare, or whatever, sometimes to my sister-in-law, and I go to work. After work I go get him and go home. I work at a restaurant and I'm in there for just the busy times. So after the lunch work I go home. I make food, clean the house, do those things around the house and then I go back to work in the evening. My boyfriend (the baby's father) watches Daniel in the evening. I come back home at night, 10 or 11:00 and go to sleep. The next day, back again. I do this for five or six days a week. I lasted a year and a half with not working when Daniel was born, but it was really hard without money." Thus, Sophia, at 19, described a typical day for her, a young Latina high school dropout.

Frequent changes of schools, seven schools in 11 years, enabled Sophia's lack of proficiency in English and reading to go unchecked even though all of these seven schools were in three adjacent school districts. According to a teacher who had known her in two different schools, Sophia was Limited in English Proficiency (LEP). Her communication level in English was good at the conversational level, but was not adequate for high school academic-level learning. There were no ISAT scores recorded for Sophia, and she did not remember ever taking the ISAT even though she was enrolled at the time they were given.

According to Sophia, her grades all through school had been "pretty good, even in high school." She liked school, and "I really liked math," she said, "but I couldn't get the reading level that good. That's the only problem I had, and sometimes I didn't really pay attention because there were a lot of things going through my mind. And school is just another thing to go in. It wouldn't let me learn anything because of all the problems at my house."

Sophia claimed that if she could rewind the experience of high school she would pay more attention and ask more questions. "What I did sometimes was when I really didn't get what they [teachers] said and stuff and I knew I was going to flunk, I would just stop doing the work. Other times I wouldn't ask for help because I didn't know anyone in the class. None of my friends were there to ask, and I thought the teacher wouldn't help me, so I just didn't ask."

She also felt that the teachers did not always teach effectively because they expected the students to do the work independently without building on prior knowledge and experiences or preparing them with the skills and knowledge to do so. "Sometimes that was the problem because the teacher just gives you the book and expects you to do the job without telling you what you are supposed to do. What are you supposed to do? Just sit there? That's what I would have to do. They just expected too much sometimes."

Sophia noted a general lack of caring among most teachers, although she eventually thought of two teachers who were nice and had interesting learning activities. She liked math, and enjoyed the economics course taught at Zaragosa Alternative High School because the teacher presented the concepts in fun and interesting ways. "I really started doing my homework in that class. I wanted to keep up for some reason. It was really interesting, and something I could use. Like putting your bills together and I could see what I was going to waste in a whole year. We had to draw cartoons to help us understand words like 'merge,' and I still remember what that word means." Also, the students were allowed to work in groups and the atmosphere was more cooperative than competitive. "The teacher, the fun way she did it, was different than other teachers. The other teachers say, 'Here's the book. Do whatever you want.'"

Sophia generally hesitated to ask questions in class because by the time she got to high school she had gotten the message that teachers do not like it when students don't understand. "Sometimes my head would be hurting really bad because I was thinking really hard and trying to figure it out [a math problem] and he [the teacher] wouldn't want to explain. He would just get tired of me, I guess, asking him questions on how to do it. Maybe I expected too much." Sophia often blamed herself for failing to graduate. She was sympathetic to the burden of responsibility placed on her teachers of meeting the needs of so many students. "You're not the only one asking for help," she explained. "There's a lot more."

Sophia also noticed the difference in the way White students performed in school and concluded that, "Maybe they're just smarter. Maybe they just learn faster or get the stuff better. Most of the times when I go to school, the teachers are White. You don't see any Mexicans teaching because—I don't know why. I don't remember not even one teacher being Hispanic in any school I've been in. Not principals either."

Sophia thought that she would not find anything useful in courses such as social studies and science. She confided that she later realized that some of the information presented was useful, for instance that it would have been useful to know about the tsunami for the people living near the ocean in India and Thailand. She recalled learning about tsunamis in science but thinking that they weren't real. "Now I know, but back then I didn't know it existed. I thought things like that were only in the movies, like fake stuff."

Sophia generally had too much work after school, and few monetary resources to pay for involvement in extracurricular school activities. She was forced to stop going to school for a month during her junior year so she could work in the potato harvest. "I didn't want to quit, but I didn't have anything to do with it. I went to work for my mom for a month, but I didn't receive anything for the month because she took the money. There wasn't any point for me quitting school just for that month."

Sophia was already pregnant at the time, but intended to finish school. However, by missing a month of school she was not able to get credit for that trimester. Sophia was encouraged by the high school to enroll at Zaragosa Alternative High School to make up the credits she needed and perhaps graduate only a little later. Sophia's parents were not involved in this discussion, nor did she receive counseling services from either the high school or the alternative school about this important decision. When asked about this she said that all the high school was concerned about was getting their textbooks back, which she did the next day. "I never talked to a counselor at the high school or alternative school. I just told them I was going to Zaragosa and would try really hard, but that's about it."

The schedule at Zaragosa Alternative High School met Sophia's needs. She enjoyed the smaller class sizes and the reduced pressure of only two classes per trimester. "When I got to Zaragosa, I really did want to graduate. I tried my best and I passed all the classes while I was there. I just forgot about everything else." Sophia was able to pick up lost credits before her baby was born, and she felt she would be able to graduate on time.

After Daniel was born, Sophia returned to Zaragosa and was able to bring him with her. She enjoyed being able to check on him during the lunch break, and Sophia liked the security of knowing he was being well cared for. However, she dropped out after a month. "It was too hard. I would come to school and I would have to go back home and clean and take care of the baby. I didn't have too much time to do anything anymore. I didn't tell anyone I wasn't going to come anymore, I just didn't come back." Sophia and her boyfriend were living together by this time and Sophia had taken on serious adult roles. She was 17.

One of Sophia's teachers described her as determined and pleasant, and said, "She [Sophia] will always land on her feet because she is a hard worker. She may not graduate, but she'll make sure her child will. Sometimes the mark we make here at Zaragosa is for the next generation to do better, and sometimes that's the best we can do."

Friends were an important part of Sophia's school life. In earlier grades shyness made it difficult for her to make new friends. "The only problem getting along with other kids was when I went to another school. That was a problem and I would be shaking to go to another school because of the other people. You never know how people are going to treat you. Like at one junior high I got along with everyone and there was no one to be fighting around, but at another junior high I had a girl on my butt. She was bothering me all the time and I would always be thinking about what she was going to do instead of concentrating on school work."

It was difficult for Sophia to change schools so frequently and she was traumatized, especially when she reached junior high age, to be in a new school without close friends. "In junior high I remember not wanting to go to school. I don't like to see new people I don't know. That's hard for me because I wonder how they are going to think about me." Sophia frequently had trouble sleeping at night because she was worried about who she would eat lunch with the next day. "If you didn't have the same lunch [period] with your friends, then you would be just walking around by yourself. I wouldn't even eat. With whom am I going to eat? Where am I going to sit? It was like that at school. Different lunches for different trimesters. I would be starving when I got home because I didn't have any friends to eat with. It didn't feel good eating by yourself."

By the time Sophia made the transition to Zaragosa Alternative High School, friends became less of a concern. "I didn't have as many friends at Zaragosa, but it didn't really matter because I was really trying to get my work done so everything would go good and stuff." She did attend the high school graduation ceremony to watch her old friends and classmates receive their diplomas. "I felt so bad about it. I didn't even want to go, but I had to because my sister-in-law was graduating. I wasn't going to ruin it for her. She was really happy. All my friends just looked at me and didn't say anything. It made me feel really bad about it, and it made me think about it a lot."

Sophia was one of seven children. Her parents divorced when she was only six, with her dad taking custody of the children. The youngest child was one year old at the time. Both of Sophia's parents were described by her as distant emotionally and, often, physically. She said there was little in the way of a support system, but the siblings did look after each other and themselves. "My mom's kind of psycho, you know. She's crazy. She just starts saying bad words at you and says things that aren't true. Sometimes I think that other people don't say bad things about us, but she does—to our faces. Wow. That's our mom and she's saying bad things. What are other people going to think?"

After the divorce, Sophia's mom married again and had four more children. As Sophia's brothers and sisters got older, they gradually left their father's house, which now included a stepmother and three more children. As soon as one of the kids became a discipline problem Sophia said that her dad sent them to live with their mother in a neighboring community. Sophia's mother took the children back, but according to Sophia, she ruled with punishment. When Sophia became pregnant, she did not tell her mother until after she had transferred to the alternative school.

Sophia's mother left school after fifth grade to work as a farm laborer. Sophia's father never attended school. Her dad encouraged Sophia to graduate, but her mom saw the need for the kids to work and contribute to the family financially. Of 11 children, only Sophia's older sister had graduated. There are 6 children still at home, but "they are going wild." Sophia was never into gangs, and had no criminal involvement, but worried about her brothers and sisters getting into trouble with the law. She was the one counseling the younger siblings to make better choices, although Sophia admitted they probably won't listen to her. "I tell my sister to not to pay so much attention to her friends because sometimes you are with them too much and you don't focus on what really matters—school. Focus on doing your homework and not messing around. But really I don't know if she will listen. I didn't. My sister tells me that I'm her favorite because I understand, but I don't think I do. I didn't do all the things she's doing right now. I don't know why she is going wild, but I want to help her."

Sophia thought her mother had too many children to take care of and did not want to make that mistake herself. "Forget it. You don't have time or money for them so why make them? I'm just going to have the ones that I can actually take care of and look after, and I'm not going to be like my mom and just pay attention to her boyfriend. She doesn't care about anybody else. My mom says stuff like, 'Yeah, you'd rather have a baby than graduate.' But I just stay quiet because it was kind of her fault."

Sophia worried about what other people thought about her. "Some people think dropouts are not smart enough to graduate. I know what they are thinking, like I'm stupid and stuff. I want to do something for myself and be a better person, but right now I don't have anything. It's hard. A dropout is a person that didn't finish. That's all. Life is harder for you, I think." Sophia vacillated between believing she was not smart and believing that she had done an amazing job of taking care of her family.

Sophia's boyfriend, who did not graduate either, was supportive of her dream to either graduate or get a GED. They had not yet translated that support into an action plan. "My boyfriend told me that I can still make it. I'll either graduate or get a GED, one of those things. It doesn't matter which one. I just want something and not to feel like I'm dumb or something. I want to have it so when I apply for a job and when they say, 'Did you graduate?' I can say, 'Yes.'"

Sophia was not afraid of work, but would like a better job, one that required less physical stress. "Not graduating wasn't a good thing because it's really hard to get hired and even harder in the winter. I got a newspaper to look for employment, and I was reading about what you need for the jobs. Then it said you have to have a GED or graduate from school. So for that job I just said, 'Forget it. I didn't finish school. I didn't graduate. I don't have anything.' It's hard. If you graduate it's a little bit better. But then it's still really hard when there are no jobs."

When she was younger, Sophia used to say she wanted to be a teacher, but later gave up the idea. She also felt that getting the money for college would be impossible. Sophia's boss had just found out she liked to cook and offered to let her try it at the restaurant, so she was considering accepting that offer. "But, I really don't have anything special that I really want to do. I just want to graduate and have a good job."

"When I got this restaurant job, I wasn't happy about going back and forth to work at just the busy times. But I filled out a lot of applications at a lot of places and never even got called or anything. It's a hard job, washing dishes and lifting heavy boxes, and the boss doesn't want you to be resting at all. He wants me to be going and going. I got really mad yesterday and I wanted to quit. But if I quit, then I don't get anything from it. I don't get another job right away, so now I have to stay until he tells me to go. It's just hard. I'm still there because I know I can do it, but I want to get a better job and to get paid better."

Sophia's day revolved around work, and taking care of her son and boyfriend and the little home they shared. She felt fulfillment in that role. The relationships she valued were the priorities. "I wouldn't change having my son. I couldn't even say that. It's just that sometimes it seems like me doing everything. But then I think, 'I can't believe I can actually do all this.'"

CHAPTER FIVE

Case Studies

LATINO YOUTH EXPERIENCES IN AND OUT OF SCHOOL

ARMANDO

"In schools they judge you before they know you. Schools treat Hispanics different."

As the youngest of 18 children, and the only child living in Idaho, a typical day for Armando revolved mainly around helping his aging parents. "Lately I get up at 8:00 in the morning and go look for work. I spend time with my son when I have the time, and that's mostly every day. I go out, but I don't go looking for trouble. I help my dad because his health is bad. He can't walk very far without getting tired. We live in the country, so I usually burn the garbage and shovel the snow. I take my mom places. My dad's been sick for about six years. He was only given five years to live at first, but he's lived past that pretty well. He even looks like he's getting better. He's on disability because he can't work. You can't do much with only $672 a month, so my mom has to work and it's hard for her too. With one driver you can't do it. One needs to go one way, the other the other way. We did have two cars but mine is in the shop right now. My mom doesn't know how to drive a standard, so I have to drive her around. That's about all I do now." He worries about what will happen to his mother if his dad dies.

When Armando dropped out of school at 19, he had only 11 of the 40 credits needed for graduation. Before ninth grade, his report cards showed mostly Cs and Ds. Because of his poor grades in junior high, Armando was excluded from sports and he gave up trying to be involved in extracurricular activities from that point on. Outside influences seemed to keep Armando from focusing on school work; however, he always told himself that he would do better next time.

"The next year I said I'm going to at least try this time, and I couldn't because too much stuff was going on. I shouldn't use that as an excuse, but that's the way it was. When you have things going on in your head you just can't concentrate right." Armando felt he would not have lasted in school as long as he did if alternative schools weren't available. The flexibility and scheduling differences enabled him to concentrate on fewer things, but for Armando that worked only up to a point. Eventually the difficulties of his life were too overwhelming and as he put it, he "messed up."

Armando took most of the blame for his school failure. Armando regrets not graduating with his class and remembers feeling bad while attending the ceremony and watching friends walk across the stage and receive the hand-shake and diploma. "I was sad because I should have been up in that line, but I had to mess up and it's what I chose. It's not that I'm a bad person; it's just that I made bad choices." Armando said he was disorganized in school, and often did the work and then lost it or forgot to hand it in. However, he did pass two of the three components of the ISAT, which has a 10th-grade level competency. "When we did the ISATs, I banked two of my scores, so that was a positive thing right there. I didn't think I would do that good. My English I still need to pass, but I banked the reading and math." He did not expect to pass and now believes he could have done even better if he would have gone into the tests believing he could do it. His weakness was English and he complained that he just was not interested in learning about it. "I can't do the pronouns, verbs, adjectives, and stuff. I can't understand where you would put one or the other in sentences. I can't identify the adverbs or whatever it is you have to identify."

Armando found English teachers to be "cold" and he responded more to the teachers' attitudes than to the particular subject matter. Armando felt that there were times when the attitudes of teachers were racially biased. "In schools they judge you before they know you. Schools treat Hispanics different. They do. When I was at New Castle there were teachers that would just let you do your work on your own because you were Hispanic. Some of the teachers will help you, but some don't. I just kind of accept that's the way it is. You can't change it." The teachers at Zaragosa Alternative High School had helped Armando, he admitted, although he did not appreciate it at the time. He felt that at Zaragosa the "teachers cared about you and what your life was like. At junior high school no one did that. They didn't even know me."

The best teachers, according to Armando, "will stick by you, care about you, and are not going to quit on you." One-to-one communication and spending time were seen as ways teachers showed they really care. Only one teacher at the junior high Armando attended really helped him. "She got mad at me and pulled me out of class one day and talked to me. She put some sense into my head and helped me out in class to bring up my grade. She wouldn't kick me out of class when I wanted her to," he laughed.

At Zaragosa, "you have a little more slack. The principal cares. He's an excellent principal and counselor, too. He's helped me a lot on my stuff, and I could tell him anything. You can look at him like a peer. I was having trouble with my fiancée, and he told me 'If you really love this girl, you aren't going to be putting her through what you're putting her through right now. You shouldn't act the way you are with her. You shouldn't be so jealous.' At the time he was saying it, it went in one ear and out the other, but it still stuck in my head. As the days went by I would think about it and I started doing what he told me to do and we got back together. That's what he put me into."

The worst teachers "were just there to show you once. If you asked them for help they would barely give it to you. Most of the teachers would just give you the work and say, 'Here, you can do it. Read the chapters.' How teachers could help me out is to be more supportive. There are a lot of kids who struggle, like the kids from Mexico. They come here to get an education that they can't get over there and yet some of the teachers are not willing to help them learn English. In the other town I lived in they pulled the kids out and really teach you, but in some places they don't do that."

Armando mentioned that he got more involved in learning when there were group activities and fun projects. He insisted, however, that most of the problems he had in school were his own fault. "You've got to be willing to learn and at the time I was not willing to learn. You can't help someone that's not willing."

Armando's best memories of school revolved around relationships with peers. He admitted that he had missed out by being distracted by family and friend problems instead of focusing on school. In eighth grade he was caught drinking and ran from the police in what turned into a high-speed chase. He wrecked the car, and luckily only slightly injured himself and his female passenger. That incident was his first brush with the law, but others followed. "They put me into alternative school after eighth grade because the principal said I was too old to be at the junior high. There were other kids older than me who stayed, but I think they didn't want me because of wrecking the car and all that. My grades weren't even down; they were C average. I had passed my classes. My parents went to talk to the principal, but he just said I was too old to be there anymore."

In high school there were incidents with a rival gang. Armando had three small dots on the skin between his thumb and index finger, a gang symbol for unity. He admitted to gang involvement at one time, but after being arrested for drug possession and having no one in the gang help him out, he changed his mind. "That was my worst mistake right there, getting into something like that." Armando observed that what he thought was a group of people he could count on was an illusion. He felt that his gang involvement was not serious. He claimed that the worst thing anyone ever did to him at school was smear nachos all over the inside of his car. "Right now I don't talk to nobody, not the people I used to hang around with or other people. Now it's mostly all White kids and kids from other countries that I talk to. I don't pay attention to the guys around here no more because they're the ones who got me into trouble. So I'm trying to stay away."

Armando had several girlfriends, and girl problems, including one incident where the mothers of two girls who were fighting over him got into a fight. "We had about six cops over there at the alternative school because of that fight. It was a good thing that the principal wasn't there because he was pretty mad the next day. He called us down and told us he didn't want any of that there, because if it happened one more time he'd put us in jail. I guess one of the girls wanted to fight one of the moms. It was pretty crazy. I was outside the building and they wouldn't let me in because they said I would make it worse. So I stayed outside. That was OK with me."

Problems with his relationships sidetracked Armando from his studies and resulted in at least two years of no progress in school. "The last year in school I didn't gain no credit whatsoever. I was having problems at home, and my fiancée and I were splitting up. I couldn't concentrate on it [school] like I was supposed to. I wasn't in trouble; I was just not doing my work. I was there just to go to school and not learn nothing. That's when I started thinking I should just drop out."

Armando grew up in poverty and lived in a high-poverty area. He missed most of second grade while migrating with his parents from one seasonal crop to another, so he had to repeat that grade. "We were always moving around and going to Washington so my parents could get something going, picking apples or whatever. They couldn't get no jobs around here." He often missed several weeks of school during the harvest season to earn money to help out his parents, who eventually settled in this area and worked as farm laborers. "My parents really wanted me to graduate or get a GED because they never got it. My mom dropped out when she was in seventh grade and my dad was kicked out for fighting. He was a troublemaker," Armando laughed. "I guess they don't want those."

Armando's father was dying from emphysema and had been quite ill for the past five years. "My dad got sick working on a farm with chemicals and all that stuff. He doesn't want me to go through the same thing as he did." Armando did not really know his older siblings, who live as far away as the East Coast. He remarked that he has some nieces and nephews that he has never met. Without other family members around, Armando relied on his parents for financial support. "They have helped me pay for my car; helped me get what I need, clothes; put a roof over my head. So, I think I would like to help them back, too. They think an education would be a lot more helpful to my life than what I have now. Now all I can work in is factories, plants, farms, and dairies, like my dad did before he got sick. My parents didn't get to graduate, but some of my aunts and uncles did. I think some of my stepbrothers have graduated because they have really good jobs and big houses and stuff, so I imagine that they graduated."

Armando's parents encouraged him to stay in school, which he did despite a lack of connection with school and difficulty juggling seasonal work and school. "They want me to get a real nice job, be a steady person, and grow up different than they grew up. They don't want me to be in trouble like I am now because that's how my dad was. Now I have been back and forth into jail. I tried to straighten things out; it didn't work and I just got in deeper and deeper."

Armando had dreamed of a job in law enforcement, but felt that was over because of his criminal record. "I would like to learn more about the law. I would like to ride with a cop, because that's how you start. But before I do that I don't want them to think I'm just trying to brown nose them for points. I want to get off probation and then tell them I'm interested. That's going to take a couple of years, but I've had that goal for a long time so maybe it will happen."

He was also interested in joining the Job Corps, but was concerned about leaving his mother and his sick father. Armando had also become a father and did not want to leave his son and fiancée, not even for six weeks. At one point after his son was born, Armando and his fiancée had an apartment together, but found that keeping steady jobs that would pay all the bills was more than the young couple could manage. The stress of their struggling relationship caused the two to part when the baby was a little over a year old. His fiancée eventually moved back in with her parents and Armando moved back in with his. Later, the two resolved some of their differences and were making plans to get back together as soon as one or both of them had steady work and they could afford the costs of running a household.

Armando realized that part of the problem between him and his parents was a lack of communication. He doesn't want to make the same mistake with his son. "Well, my parents never really talked to me about what to do or give [sic] me advice until it was too late. That's what I want to do. I want to put something in my son's life that I didn't get in mine, and hopefully keep him out of trouble."

Armando believed in the importance of a high school diploma but he was also aware of the additional burden of trying to secure a good education and good employment in the face of racism by some school personnel and employers. At the junior high school, Armando lost interest in education and felt teachers did not care to even know who he was. Since he perceived school personnel had no interest in his school success, he described the process as one of losing interest and then getting into progressively more trouble. Armando was aware of societal expectations for a completion certificate of high school, but he did not really think it would be useful to him except as something to brag about. However, he also stated that when a person quits school to work full-time they are gaining money for the immediate time, but losing out by not being qualified for a better job in the future.

Armando appreciated the efforts of school personnel at the alternative school, but it was a case of too little too late: "When I dropped out of alternative, the principal talked to me about it. He gave me the opportunity to come back if I wanted to, but, I don't know." "To tell you the truth," he then remarked, "if I do get my diploma or a GED, around here it won't do me no good. Maybe if I moved to a bigger city, but around here they look too much at your history and they judge you. Like when you go into Wal-Mart. There are a couple of workers who mostly watch the Hispanics when they are walking around in groups. They look at us and they always seem to be seeing if we're doing something wrong. They make us feel uncomfortable by following us around."

At one time he stated, "I don't think you have to graduate from high school to be a success, but maybe sometimes I believe that. I do know some people who work as supervisors in plants and stuff, and they got real good money and they don't have a high school diploma. They started out low and ended up big." Later on he recalled hearing that the GED doesn't really do any good and it is better to have a high school equivalency certificate. "To me, though, I've always liked to work in the plants and stuff, so I don't know if getting it [GED or high school equivalency] would be worth it. Well, it would make me look good."

Armando saw dropping out as a long process that started in seventh grade. "I would like to go back and finish school the right way, but I would have to go all the way back to junior high to make the changes, to change all that stuff to where I could have graduated at the right time. *Back to the Future, Part 4*," he laughed. He understood that for him, dropping out was an accumulation of events that snowballed into an avalanche of overwhelming proportions. "Right now I don't feel too good because I'm not working. I tried working full-time and going to school, but that only lasted four days. The last day we went to watch a drug program, and I fell asleep. I slept through the whole thing. I hadn't had any sleep for four days. They said I could have had a breakdown or something."

If Armando had known what his life was going to be like at age 20, he would have done things differently. He thought dropping out would bring freedom, but instead he is now in a place that has fewer choices than he could have imagined. "You can't tell a person what to do, but you can explain all the reasons not to drop out and what can happen. A lot of people are curious about what things are like, but there are some things you don't want to try. I thought dropping out would be real cool because I was free not to go to school and not messing with teachers. But when it came down to it, there's really nothing to do. Once you do it [drop out], it's hard to go back. You think you're going to be independent, but it's more stress on you and you're not going to get the education you need.

"I think other people look at dropouts as bad people. I think they say, 'Yeah, he's not going to be good for nothing.' But it's not all about that. There are times when you have to drop out. Some of the parents don't make that much money to support what they need to live on and when the potato season comes sometimes their kids have to drop out of school to work. They need to help their families survive. It's not about dropping out because they want to. For me, sometimes I think it was because I just didn't want to go to school anymore. But if I didn't want to go to school, why was I still there for so long?"

CESAR

"I just quit trying. I wasn't interested anymore."

Cesar was 17 and would soon be 18. He was at the county courthouse, where he was being released from a month-long detention in the county jail for a probation violation, having failed a urinalysis. The urinalysis had been given at the request of Cesar's mother, who had told the probation officer that she suspected Cesar was using drugs.

Before Cesar's arrest, a typical day would entail sleep because he worked the night shift. "I would be sleeping all day and then wake up and get ready to go to work again. That was practically it. Just sleep and go to work. I live at home with my parents, so some days I would not go right to sleep and I would help my dad work on a car or help him in some other way. But most days I would sleep. In the summer sometimes I would hang out with my friends or go play soccer, but I never missed a night of work because of that. I always showed up for work on time."

Cesar dropped out of high school in February. He had completed the coursework to be eligible for 10th-grade status; however, he should have been in 11th grade. When he left school, Cesar was 17. At Hagerstown High School, his grades were poor, with primarily Ds and Fs in core subjects. Cesar was not able to play soccer at school that year, a sport he excelled in, because he had at least two Fs in core subjects [English and math].

Cesar's academic decline began in middle school, when he "lost interest" in doing the work and became overwhelmed by the demands homework put on his after-school time. "Before when I was little I would get good grades, but in middle school, I don't know. I just quit trying. I just wasn't interested anymore."

Grade school was a successful experience for Cesar, but middle school was harder and high school academics were so overwhelming that he gave up trying. "I wouldn't turn in the work," he admitted. "I never really even did the homework. When they gave me homework I would just get home and put it off until later, and later, and later. And I would end up not doing it. Sometimes I would try to do it, but a lot of the time I didn't understand what they wanted." Cesar's older brother, still living at home, was a successful student, but Cesar did not solicit his help. Once he got old enough to work, shortly after turning 16, Cesar began to think more and more about working to earn a living instead of going to school.

Cesar's disinterest in school translated into increasing tardiness, truancy, and neglect of homework. Because of poor grades and attendance since beginning high school, Cesar had lost credits. He was also getting into fights with rival "gang members" affiliated with the school. "It was basically just Mexicans fighting Mexicans," he disclosed. The vice principal related that there was "a problem in the school with rival gangs and fights," but he described Cesar as a "nice boy who was quiet, respectful, and a good soccer player." He expressed surprise when told that Cesar had not played soccer for the school the last year he attended because of his grades. "Usually the coaches go after the kids who contribute to the team," he remarked.

No one at the school contacted Cesar's parents about his decline and they were unaware that he was a year behind in credits when he got into a fight that resulted in a battery charge and jail time. This was the first direct experience with law enforcement for Cesar, and the weekend in juvenile detention exacerbated his mounting problems. Cesar believed that if he went back to school, things would not change and, because he lost credits, he would not graduate with his peer group.

In Cesar's opinion, his main academic difficulty was teachers. They assigned a lot of homework that did not seem useful to Cesar, gave few explanations and no individual help. They were condescending to students who asked questions or did not understand what to do, and they did not connect on a personal level with the students. One teacher, the worst according to Cesar, would give them a packet of work to complete. When they had questions she'd say, "Well, look through the packet. You've got to read it." Cesar didn't understand what she wanted him to do and felt she didn't care. He said, "That's why I was the student who was mostly goofing around instead of doing what I was supposed to. School didn't really attract my attention so that when the teacher was talking I wouldn't listen. I think it's real common for kids my age. My friends had that same problem and they dropped out."

Lectures really turned him off and Cesar understood that he learned better when someone showed him. But few courses provided that type of experience. He did find computers, debate, drama, and speech to be useful and could articulate how he learned. He was not afraid to get up in front of a group to present or perform and found this a way he liked to learn. For Cesar, if the learning was not something he believed was "useful" it was hard to put time and effort into the task.

Cesar believed that schools could be more supportive by providing after-school tutoring programs and asserted that he would have taken advantage of it. He took the 10th-grade ISAT, passing the math and language parts, but not the reading section. "It was pretty long, but it was all right. I wasn't nervous. They said it counted to graduate, but I didn't really pay attention to that. I just did it."

While incarcerated for failing the urinalysis, Cesar attended GED (General Education Diploma) preparation classes provided by the detention center. The one-to-one tutoring and encouragement helped him realize that he did have strong math skills and it was possible for him to get a GED. At the high school he had been doing poorly in his math courses and Cesar now believed that this was because the teacher was not explaining the information in a way that Cesar could understand it. He felt that most of the courses in high school were taught by people who did not care for the students. He could only think of one "best teacher" and that person would show the students how to do the work, explain it step-by-step, and check for understanding before moving on.

Cesar was socially inclined and sought experiences that enabled interaction with peers. In school this meant participation in soccer and drama; out of school it meant hanging out with friends. He was involved in what school officials saw as a gang; however, Cesar claims that it wasn't real gang involvement. "Like one day if you were wearing blue pants and a blue shirt, and the kids would say that you're South Side because you were wearing all blue. I mean, there are gangs around here, but this was kids who think they are in, that they represent or whatever. But they're not really in a gang. It's just kids messing around."

The messing around escalated to the point that Cesar was involved in numerous fights. In the last one, which happened just off school grounds after school last spring, Cesar was arrested and charged with battery. The other individual was not charged "because he didn't fight back. He just took it." It was after the subsequent weekend in the detention center that Cesar disclosed to his parents his problems at school. He convinced them that staying in school would result in more fighting and more incarceration, so they agreed to let him drop out and go to work. He immediately found a job and began taking on an adult role. "I always had to ask my parents for this and that, and now I come in with my own money. That's an advantage because they don't have all the weight of the household on them. I just kept some and contributed some."

Soccer was still an important part of Cesar's life and even though the school denied him the opportunity to play, he was able to join an adult summer soccer league. His older brother was also a member of the soccer league and that helped Cesar stay connected with family members who were very important to Cesar. After school started in the fall, Cesar became lonely because he had lost his social network. Most of his friends were still in school and when school was out for the day, he would be getting ready to go to work. "I was always at work, so I kind of felt left out. Sometimes I think I should have stayed in school because now I don't hang out with people my age anymore."

Cesar's new friends, older young adults, were not good influences, and after dropping out of school he became involved in the use of methamphetamines. Cesar feels that the 30-day detention he recently served gave him time to rethink his choice of friends, but he has not yet decided to disconnect completely from the older group who got him into methamphetamine drug use. "It will be easy not to do the meth, because I wasn't hooked on it or anything. I was just messing around. That's the lucky part. I just have to stay away from it and if those guys are my real friends then they shouldn't have me be around it or even talk about it. They should support me and help me with that decision. That's what I've been thinking about while I was in there [juvenile detention]."

Cesar described his family as having a strong work ethic and said that everyone who can work does so with vigor. The family immigrated from Mexico to Idaho 14 years ago and many family members have worked in the dairy industry ever since. Neither of Cesar's parents graduated and both had experienced difficulty with school in Mexico. They were sympathetic to Cesar's complaints about the difficulty of the work in high school. Cesar's mother did not speak English, but his father was bilingual. Cesar's parents were totally unaware that he had lost almost a year's worth of credit and that his grades were so low. They did not know about the truancy and tardies. The school had been silent on this issue. Neither parent was contacted by the school regarding Cesar's academic progress and his parents did not contact the school because to do so meant taking time off work, potentially losing one's job and the ability to take care of the family.

Cesar's parents needed to keep their employment and could not take time off work to supervise their teenage son. That priority was not groundless. According to Cesar's probation officer, Hector, if unskilled workers are sick or unable to do the job, they will be quickly replaced. This proved to be true in Cesar's case. Missing one month of work at the dairy while being incarcerated resulted in the loss of his job, even though his boss was pleased with his work ethic and would give him a good employment reference. Hector said, "If parents are required to work late or graveyard shifts, they will not be able to keep track of what their children are doing at night. If they work all day, six or seven days a week, they will not be available if the school calls. They will also have little ability to check in at the school to see if their child is making progress."

In Cesar's case, because his older siblings had been successful in school and had graduated on time, his parents had little reason to suspect he would be different. He was given a lot of trust and typically they did not question what he was doing with his friends. "My parents let me go with my friends, no problem. Sometimes I would help my dad with the cows, and if I did that, he would let me go if I asked permission." Cesar's parents had not spoken to him about their expectations for him beyond high school. "Well, they never really talked to me when I was in school. They didn't really talk that much about school. They just asked if I was doing all right and if I had any trouble, because I would get in trouble sometimes."

After his arrest for battery, Cesar explained his problems with school and fighting to his parents. They left the decision of whether to stay in school or not up to him. "My dad said he would back me up with what I wanted to do. I didn't really think they were going to let me. I thought my dad was going to make me keep going, but he said, 'We can't make you go because you won't even try and it will be a waste of your time.'"

Cesar believed in the value of getting a high school diploma, but also felt the additional pressure of needing to contribute financially to his family's economic situation. At one time he said he thought "getting an education is important. You can't get a good job if you don't have a good education." Another time he stated that with a diploma, he wouldn't have to work at a dairy. However, later on he said that if people did not like school and could go to work, then they should do that, because he was making a lot of money at the dairy and it enabled him to contribute to his family's economic survival.

Cesar noticed that both of his older siblings had graduated and they were working in manual labor jobs as nursery/landscaping laborers, so the importance that the school had placed on getting a diploma to get a better job did not match up with his reality. A good job was "something that pays a lot, but is not that much work for you. You don't come home all tired and don't want to do nothing. Like when I come home from the dairy, I just want to sleep. I would work eight hours, but I only had one day off a week. I didn't have time to do anything. I would just fall asleep. No time to even spend my money."

Cesar said he may try to get a GED in the future and that he was interested in computers. He would also like to use computer knowledge to help him become a mechanic. "When I was little I would say I wanted to be a mechanic because my dad fixes cars and I would help him out. I was interested in that. I am always helping my dad fix cars, so I know some things about that." However, he also said that his long-term plans were to work at the nursery with his sister.

Cesar was proud of the way he took on the adult role of working full-time and contributing to his family. In the six months he worked before being incarcerated, he did not miss a day or complain about the rigorous schedule of working six days a week. He liked being treated as an adult by his family. With regards to his current group of older friends, he admits that they were responsible for introducing him to methamphetamines. He felt he would not make this mistake again. Cesar did not regret the decision to drop out as much as the decision to use drugs. "I lost my job. I had a job and was making money. And now because of going into detention I lost my job. Well, I got nothing to do now." Cesar said that since he had nothing to do he would consider the GED possibility, but if another job opened up he would take that instead.

Cesar did not believe that people have control over what happens in their lives and that external influences can derail plans. "Just because you're still in high school doesn't mean you are going to graduate." He chose to put difficulties behind him and move forward, hoping things will work out in his favor. Cesar described a dropout as "someone who just wasn't doing good in school and decided to do something else instead of going through the same thing every day and not succeeding at it. It's somebody that just got tired of trying." His advice to people who want to keep students from dropping out was to get better teachers. "Ones that aren't going to just give you work, but who are going to work with you. Not just hand it out and have you do whatever. That's the biggest thing."

VICTOR

"If you want something, you've got to get it yourself."

It was Valentine's Day when Victor first arrived at the elementary school in Juniper Hills. He remembered this clearly because the second-grade class had been notified about their new classmate and had prepared valentines and candy for him. "Because the new kid was coming to school and they wanted him welcome, and that was me. I still remember it." When he was little he wanted to be a doctor. "I would always look it up and it showed that I had to do a lot of college and stuff like that, and I wanted to do it real bad. It just didn't work out. Later on, I thought I could have money without going to school."

In the end, Victor was expelled from Juniper Hills High School. He had completed his sophomore year and was 16. When he asked the principal why he was being expelled, he was told that he didn't have enough credits to graduate and he didn't need to be there anymore. Victor went home and returned to school with his father, but the principal wouldn't budge. So Victor enrolled in the alternative school to try to get enough credits to go back to the high school. At the alternative school, Victor was reprimanded several times for "disrespecting a teacher" and excessive absences. He earned additional credits at the alternative school, but the high school still would- n't take him back. So Victor enrolled in a high school (with a majority of White students) in a neighboring county. He was expelled from there for "selling marijuana and fighting." "When I was in school everybody always told me I was smart, but I always thought school was a waste of time. I thought it was too easy, and so I thought I knew everything. So I started skip- ping and whatever."

At the elementary school level, Victor's grades were all As and Bs, but by the end of 8th grade, Fs, Ds and Cs were the grades Victor received most often. His grade point average was just high enough to play high school sports. "I was pretty good," he said. Being athletic brought Victor attention and close relationships with other teammates. However, he could not recall ever talking seriously with a coach or assistant coach. "I didn't really talk to them; I just played."

"I was the student who was always trying to do his own thing. I thought selling drugs or whatever would work, but I guess not. Some of the teachers liked me. But the ones who knew I was smoking [pot] or whatever, skipping school and coming back high, I thought they were trying to get rid of me." There was no dropout prevention program at Juniper Hills High School and Victor did not visit with school counselors or teachers about his problems. "If I have problems, I don't tell anyone. I just take care of it myself."

"In this small town, the kids who do well are involved in sports or other school activities. Those that aren't involved find other things to do, and most of it isn't good," stated one of Victor's favorite teachers, Mr. C. "Victor was my best math student ever. His problem was a bad attitude and drugs." At Juniper Hills High School, Victor had already passed the 10th-grade ISAT of reading, language and math. He said he got terrible grades in class work, but did well on the ISAT tests. "I can't really concentrate on doing something for a long period of time. I always gotta be moving around." He said he enjoyed being the "class clown," "skipping school," and "driving around town in his truck."

Victor was convinced that it was too late for him to get a high school diploma. "I'm already 18 now and I don't want to go back. I'd only be in 10th or 11th grade. I'd be the oldest. I never dropped out; it's not something I wanted, but I was messed up and got myself into trouble. It's my fault, anyways. To tell you the truth, I was excited to see how it was going to be to start working and have money and stuff, a job and a paycheck. But when I lost the job, I didn't have no money or nothing. I didn't have anything to fall back on."

Victor did regret not succeeding in school. "I was in Juvey [juvenile detention center] while everyone was graduating. I looked at the newspaper and, you know, my best friend got the Bill Gates Scholarship. I was thinking, 'Man, look at me. I'm over here locked up and he's over there getting scholarships. He's going to be something.' I was just stressing out. I could have been there too."

Victor liked living in Juniper Hills, even if it was a small town. He enjoyed knowing most people and being known by them. He enjoyed being able to walk to school or the store, or just around town to see his friends. However, "now it's boring because everyone's still in school. It's not fun being home. I'd rather be in school and doing something, or at least working." He admitted to focusing on his friends while in school. "I was just screwing off. I didn't really want to be in school."

Victor was in trouble for fighting. Victor said of one incident, "I went from a school that had a lot of Hispanics to a school that was mostly White people." Victor claimed the White kid he fought with was "always messing with me, staring at me from far away, in a big old group. They thought I was scared or whatever. One day this kid just tells me, 'What the hell is your problem?' I don't know if he thought I wouldn't do anything or what. I got suspended for five days and when I came back I got caught with weed. I was selling it at school to make money." He said he had been selling marijuana at school for "a long time."

"The cops got involved and stuff, and so it was a little more serious. They said I could go back [to that school] in a year, but I had to go in front of the board and everything. They said my grades and everything I had done showed no reason for them to let me stay. So they basically kicked me out."

Victor partially blamed his upbringing for his fighting. "The way I was brought up, my dad always told me 'you gotta be a man and toughen up and stop crying' and stuff like that. I always felt like 'no mercy' or something like that." His parents were married at a very young age. Neither parent graduated from high school, but they encouraged Victor to stay in school and graduate. "They wanted me to go to college, but I never thought I would get that far." His parents told him that an education would make life easier and it would be easier to get a job.

"I know my parents always cared, but they didn't go to school. They were struggling, too, and they couldn't pay too much attention and help us with our homework because they were always busy." Victor felt that he was more understanding of his parent's shortcomings now that time had gone by, but when he was younger their inability to support him made him angry. Victor recalled that as far back as he could remember he would go to school upset because of his home situation. His parents fought, and it affected Victor's school performance. "I was always getting in trouble. The teacher would say, 'Well, pull out your paper. We're going to do an essay.' And I'd throw out an attitude because I was having a bad day." In middle school Victor served a lot of after-school detentions for having a negative attitude toward school work and the teachers.

When Victor was in high school his parents got divorced and he moved in with his dad. "I always liked to smoke, since I was about fifteen. It's probably because I always seen my dad do it, and I tried it and I guess I liked it, and I kept doing it." A few months later, Victor's dad was arrested on drug charges and sent to jail. "He went to jail and I didn't have nowhere to go. I couldn't find a job. I put in applications everywhere. So, I just had to stay wherever I could because my mom didn't want me back." Victor's mother was upset because he had chosen to live with his dad in the first place. After his father had been jailed, his mother did not look for Victor or check to see if he was being taken care of. When he got hungry enough to show up at her house, she sent him away. "I was only 17 and she didn't even care. I was hungry and she would say, 'What are you doing here? What do you want? You're not supposed to be here.'" Victor felt that his mother did not really care that he was living on the streets for two months and did not have anywhere to go. "I had a lot of hate for her because of that. Now I just try to block it out, but I'll never forget it."

Victor would visit his father in jail, but did not tell him what was going on at home. "My dad, he worried about me, but I would always tell him that I'm fine, that I got a job and was staying somewhere. I would just tell him that so he wouldn't worry." The bond between father and son was pretty tight. "Nobody else would go with him. I didn't want him to be alone and all the other kids were with my mom."

Victor is the oldest of the four children. The younger three were still in school and seemed to be doing well. Victor expected them to graduate. "I tell my brothers and sister to stay in school and stay out of trouble. They listen, but they're like me, they just go, 'Yeah, yeah, I'm doing all right.' If I found out one of them was doing drugs, there's nothing you can do. I would talk to them and tell them what can happen and it will just ruin things for them, but you can't make them stop. They'll probably do it even more."

When Victor's mother went to school to check on her children, she did not have a positive experience. Educators said that she was "verbally abusive" to her children, even in public. "His mother means well, but takes a negative approach when talking to and about her children," stated one of Victor's teachers. "He wanted to be like his dad and [his] dad is now in prison for dealing. Vic would tell people right out that he wanted to sell drugs like his dad. And he did."

With a large extended family in the area, Victor received advice from uncles and cousins. "I tell them that I'm looking for work and stuff because that's how they are. If you're not going to school, then you should be working. They say, 'What are you doing? Running around the streets?' It just shows they are worried. They care. They know I don't have nobody here except for my mom."

Although his mom had recently lost her job, Victor returned to her home after being released from jail. But he was sleeping on the couch. His mom refused to let him move back into his old bedroom. He was unemployed and on probation for having drug paraphernalia and resisting arrest. Victor had applied for many jobs, but there were few openings in this rural community. Because he did not have a vehicle, transportation was an issue as well. At home, his family dealt with poverty issues, including a lack of food. "My brother was hungry yesterday and I had some money so I took both of my brothers to eat. My sister didn't want to eat and my mom didn't. I just do whatever I can because I feel sorry for them because my dad's not there. The refrigerator is empty and their clothes are from last year. As soon as I get a job, I'm going to buy both my brothers some clothes. Who else is going to do it?"

Someday Victor wants an "easy job," and described that as one where you would work at a desk as opposed to being outside battling the weather. On the other hand, he commented that he liked working with his hands and felt good about being strong enough to take on roofing jobs, which he liked. He wanted to move out of his mother's house and live more independently. "As soon as I get a job I'll be happy. Well, not all the way happy, but a little bit relieved."

Victor regretted not getting along with his teachers. "I should have been like a teacher's pet or something. I would have had it easy or something. I always took the hard way, arguing with teachers, getting detentions, and getting in a lot of trouble. Because they told me not to, I would think 'What do you mean I can't do that? Watch me.' I don't know why I'm like that."

His advice to young Latinos who are considering dropping out was to stay home at night. When he was in junior high he would tell his parents he was going one place, but end up somewhere else. His parents trusted him and did not check to see where he had gone. "They trusted me for a long time. They had given me a truck and all this, and when I got kicked out [of high school] and started messing up, they took it away." Mom sold Victor's truck when he moved in with his father.

Victor felt that most of the problems he had with school originated from his own lack of interest and his inability to ask for help. He was strongly opposed to asking for help, believing it showed weakness. He did not have anyone at school he trusted enough to confide in about his family difficulties. No one at school knew that he was living on the streets for two months. This was traumatic and isolating for Victor and he had to deal with it without the help of his dad, his only support.

Victor's overall experience of dropping out put him through some rough times, but he says, "I think it just made me stronger. Because, it's like how my dad disciplined me. I'm not a weak person walking around and someone's going to walk up to me and say, 'Hey let me see your watch.' Well, it's mine. I'm keeping it. Some people would let them take the watch, because of the way they were brought up. I wouldn't let that happen at all."

Victor felt that Latino youth may have advantages over White youth because of the programs designed to help them, such as the one at a university that would enable him to become a building contractor. Victor wished he had been able to keep the roofing job he had shortly after dropping out because he liked working with his hands and learning about house construction. "I like physical work more than book learning," he added. Victor wanted to get his GED and do college entrance examinations, but had to wait because he would not be allowed to leave the county until he completed his probation. "I always figured I didn't need school, but it helps a lot."

Up until he had the experience himself, Victor always thought a high school dropout was a bum. "You know, he ain't got a job or nothing. But then, I think that's pretty much what everybody thinks. I don't want to be labeled like that, but I am. I know it's not true. Just 'cause I got kicked out of school and never went back, I'm not a bum. I'm not going to just sit around and be nothing. I like to have things and to look nice and dress nice. I won't let that happen where I'm staying on the streets, not ever again. I already know what it's like staying here and there. I didn't like it. It's not fun. You'd better go to school because if you can't even get through that, then what's going to happen to you when you get out on the street? You can't get a job or whatever. I've been there."

Victor believed that everything that happened to him was meant to happen. "I had control, but it [marijuana] was all around me. People all around me had money and they wanted to buy drugs. I had somewhere to get it, so I would make money, and I would also do it too. It just became a habit, you know. That's the way it is." Whatever the future holds, Victor was sure that he would have to make good things happen and not rely on others. "I learned that everyone is just out for themselves. No one else is going to make you happy. You've got to do it yourself. If you want something, you've got to get it yourself. No one's going to give you anything."

ENRIQUE

"He [the principal] didn't care about us, basically. He didn't see any reason for us to grow up to be something."

Talkative, with a sense of humor, Enrique spoke cautiously at first. He had lived in Juniper Hills since his parents moved there from Mexico when he was three. Enrique was described by one teacher as a "polite kid who struggled in school because of language problems," by another teacher as "a terrific classroom disruption," and by a third as "bright with tremendous potential." He described himself as a person who likes to watch others and learn from what they do. Enrique was expelled from high school when he was 16.

At the time of this study Enrique had been out of school for two years. "Right now, I'm studying [to take the GED] at home. I ain't working. Actually I'm being kind of lazy and putting it off. I was working in the onions, but now I'm just trying to take a little vacation. But I need to start studying." In reality, Enrique worked full-time for only two months after leaving school. He had frequent absences and said he had little in common with the other workers, who were typically Mexican nationals. He felt like he's more American than Mexican and recalled that in elementary school people would call him names, like "spic, wetback, mojo, or whatever. But I used to lie and say I was born in the United States because I wanted to fit in."

Enrique participated in the Juniper Hills school district since kindergarten. "In kindergarten I didn't know much English," he said. "I ended up playing with the people who just spoke Spanish." He learned English later by hanging around with people who spoke English. "I just observed, you know. When I went to the middle school I struggled. The teachers were always on my back, saying, 'You should do this, and you should do that.'"

School for Enrique was something to do just to keep his parents happy. "I never saw a purpose in it. It wasn't hard; it's just that I didn't really apply myself." He was failing or had very low grades in most subjects, and even in ninth grade did not have enough credits to graduate on time. Enrique passed all of the ISAT tests, which indicates his capability, even though his class grades reflected a student who was failing almost every course. He found most of what was presented in school useless. "You can have knowledge, but you need knowledge in something that pays you. That's what it's all about."

Enrique admitted that he didn't get along with most of the teachers. According to one teacher, Enrique had a bad reputation and according to another teacher, "most of the teachers are afraid of him." The teacher that Enrique named as "the best" remarked that Enrique was not strong in academic skills, but was smart and had abilities. However, he preferred acting up in class and keeping the other students entertained while "driving the teachers crazy." Enrique remarked at the end of the interview that he didn't "achieve anything in high school except having teachers not like me."

Even though teachers, administrators, and other school employees noticed that Enrique had not been putting forth effort in school for several years, his parents were not contacted about his lack of motivation and poor academic performance until just prior to the expulsion in his junior year of high school. That was when he became a "persistent behavior problem" and acquired the reputation among teachers as a "drug dealer." "He didn't work, but he always had a lot of money. You figure it out," suggested one educator.

Another teacher disclosed that Enrique's older brother excelled in both sports and academics. By that teacher's estimation, Enrique did not measure up to what his brother could do, so he quit trying in about ninth grade. "Enrique had no way of bringing academic skills to himself and he wasn't good in sports like his brother had been, so he made a name for himself in other ways that weren't so good." Enrique still wanted to follow in his brother's footsteps. He claimed that at some point he will probably get some business education in college like his brother was doing. "Since my brother has been through it, he can probably help me out."

"In high school I just found it was time to have fun, you know, just kick back with some friends. That's about it. Now and then I would do some work, but after a while I just started having interests that were out of school. I was not really playing sports or anything, so goals didn't really matter to me." Enrique described one of his friends, a White male from a poor family, as someone who was fun to be around and who acted "Hispanic." "Here, you gotta be acting White for some teachers, but you got White kids acting Mexican. They're always the kids with the really White names, too [laughs]."

As Mexican immigrants, Enrique's parents communicated mostly in Spanish. In Mexico, neither parent had finished school. Enrique also had two uncles who were employed in the field of education. Enrique's younger siblings had done well in school so far.

Enrique's dad strongly supported staying in school and getting an education. Enrique's parents told him that school will help him in life. "It's better to be in school because work is hard and school is easier." His parents thought it was important to take advantage of education. Enrique recalled his father telling him that school would "help you in life to get more money. They see it like that. My dad had to work in Mexico so he didn't get to finish school over there." Enrique's dad would rather see him study than work in a low-paying job.

Enrique was on probation for drug possession with intent to sell. He stated, "I find it kind of funny, though, because I'm better off than what I would have done in this school [Juniper Hills High School]. The GED program wouldn't have even looked at me if I had graduated." Enrique had been accepted into an intervention program for at-risk youth that paid students to complete GED requirements and get prepared to enter college. The program paid the expenses to stay in college dorms and had an eating allowance. However, Enrique would not be allowed to begin until he successfully completed his probation. He recognized the seriousness of his situation, especially that he had just turned 18 and if he got into trouble again he may do prison time.

Enrique quickly found out by working in the summer that work was hard and the money didn't go very far. "When I worked, then that made me realize that I needed to get back into school. That should be my job instead of me working for $5.15 an hour. I told myself that school is a good thing. So after summer I wanted to go back to school and I did, but once I got back it was the same old thing and I was bored."

"I mean we live in a little town right here. There's nothing to do. The only things that people look forward to are school, games, and things like that. So this little town has a lot do to with it [boredom]. This is a small town and some people do bad stuff because there's nothing else to do." Enrique remarked that if people really wanted to change things for kids who drop out, they would support programs that gave young people more positive things to do, such as sports. He felt that kids had too much free time and in a small town that meant trouble. He also suggested that there needed to be more role models for younger kids to emulate, "because the White people don't want us to make it. We have to look out for ourselves because they ain't going to look out for us."

Enrique described the community members as being two types of people: those who graduated from Juniper Hills and were still involved in the activities surrounding the school, and those who didn't get involved and felt uncomfortable going to watch sports events even if their children were participating. "The way I look at it, everything is going downhill. People don't vote and it's like they don't want to waste money on this town. I want to leave this town and go and do better things. I ain't like the others around here. I'm beyond all that."

When asked about the circumstances surrounding his school expulsion, Enrique spoke at length about the high school principal. He complained that teachers and school administrators in rural communities do not stay. "You expect them to stay longer than they do so people will get to know and trust them. He [the principal] started out pretty cool so we could get to trust him. But it was just a role, you know. I didn't like him."While still in school, Enrique had heard a rumor that the principal had a list of names and was in the process of going down the list and expelling Latino students. "And that's what he did. Maybe if he would have gone about it in a different way it would have turned out differently. Maybe if he would have connected with me, I obviously would have done something better and it would have benefited him as far as being a principal. But that would have been hard and he wanted it easy. He saw us as a waste of his time."

The day Enrique was expelled was anti-climactic. "I don't really even remember it. I got my paper to sign out; I got the teachers to sign because I was going to the alternative school. It wasn't like, 'Yeah. You're kicked out. Go home.' It wasn't like that. It was more like I was transferring. So then I left. I wasn't really surprised because he [the principal] always called me into his office. He acted like he was trying to help me by sending me to the alternative school, but he just wanted me out of his school. I'm sure the principal was laughing at me. And, over there [at the alternative school] I didn't last long either. It was way more strict. I missed three days and I was out."

Enrique went on to describe the condescending manner in which the principal at Juniper Hills, the regular high school, would discipline students. The incident that really astounded Enrique was when the principal called him into his office and then showed Enrique his paycheck. "I was thinking, 'Why are you showing me that?' You know he was kind of rubbing it in, because this is a small town and a lot of Hispanics and he was White. I'm not stupid. I know what he was trying to say. How does he know what I'm going to make in a year or when I grow old. I didn't care what he makes. He doesn't care about us, basically. He didn't see any reason for us to grow up and be something. Our stuff is limited straight out and it has to do with politics. So I didn't like him."

After that incident, Enrique expressed his disgust openly. He said some teachers told him not to be offended and that it was "just politics." He remarked, "I honestly can't say exactly what they meant, but what I think they meant was that he was Republican and this is Idaho. They don't care about us Mexicans. We're a minority. And Democrats, they say they care, but in the long run they don't either. We're just out here on our own. Look what we have right here: a bunch of Hispanics. Republicans just see us as slaves, you know. They pay us minimum wage. We're just like slaves to them; they don't care."

Enrique felt that the principal and some of the teachers were just doing their job, and then they would go back home and forget about the kids at Juniper Hills High School. They wanted kids to act a certain way, and if a kid was an individual, he wasn't accepted. "They want everybody to be in a box and do what they're told to do, and I don't like that. I mean, the founding fathers were White, so that's how it is right here. I mean, I guess sometimes you find a good teacher, but it's just when it gets bad that they [teachers] start acting like they really care. This is how it is, in my opinion."

There were a few teachers that did care, according to Enrique. "There was a teacher right over there [pointing] that tried to help me out; gave me a planner and this and that, but these other ones they just act like they care. It's mostly just a big front. They have to play the part." However, he said that he was partially to blame for his failure in school. "I didn't apply myself, so there's no need to blame the school. It was all on me because I didn't do the work. I was asking for it. I thought I was smart without doing the work. When my dad came to parent-teacher conferences, Mrs. M. tried to help me out, but there are limits to what teachers can take because I didn't really use her help. And I guess that's why she quit on me."

Enrique pointed out Mr. E. as an example of what a good teacher should be. "He gave me some insights, I guess you could say. A different view, that's what he had. He was his own person and more respectful with everybody. He was never a person to be sleazy and talk about you behind your back, and he would just concentrate on you when it comes to class work. He would always have a conversation about something useful; it wasn't a bunch of trash like, 'Oh, what happened at the game.' It was educational. He was real calm. He used to pull me aside and we'd have real conversations. He seemed more like a professor than a teacher, and he would help me understand a lot of things. He told me I had the potential to do whatever I want."

Enrique was expelled from Juniper Hills High School because, according to his conversation with the principal, he was a "bad influence" and he didn't have enough credits to graduate on time. "He tried to make it seem like I was a ringleader. But it's not my fault that kids want to look like me or whatever. I didn't really see it, but that's how he made it out to be." Overall, other than one or two teachers, Enrique didn't feel he had any backup against accusations of gang involvement and drug dealing. "When tough times came they didn't really go through the effort [to advocate for him]."

Enrique spoke at length about the drug problem in Juniper Hills and other little towns like it. He was convinced that drugs were on the streets for a reason and that they were a way of controlling poor people and keeping them in their place. "Everything is all planned out. It's like a chess game.

They [drug dealers] use the pawns and like the cops, and it's all planned out. It's mostly to make money and usually the minorities do it [use the drugs], so who benefits from that? You have people making money out of other people's misery. That's the sad thing." Enrique claimed that one of his future goals was to be able to inform people about these things and hopefully keep Latino/as from being used by drug dealers. He wanted to make an impact, especially on the lives of younger people.

"I realized how everybody wants to make money off people. I went into it, and I observed. I'm not going to be specific about what I saw, but it gave me a whole new crowd of people to watch and I knew I wasn't going to do it [drugs] no more. While I was using I saw some things. People were like puppets. So if they want it, they got to do what someone else says. That's how the streets are. They were using me. The cops say they want it off the streets, but then why do they give it to someone if they give them information? That's how it is. Trust me. Well, they don't necessarily give it, but they make sure the person gets it. They say they want information, but they don't want information; they want guinea pigs. And the dealers, they are using young kids out there. They want to get the young ones; they don't make the same quantity [profit] from older people. They make that stuff seem cool for a reason. It's all planned out."

Enrique was candid about his past police record, and asserted that he didn't see any reason to deny it. "If I did it, I did it for a reason. I have too much pride to deny it. I ain't that weak. I see people do something and deny it, and I look down on them. When you do something, you do it for a reason."

After he finished his probationary period, Enrique wanted to go to college, but did not want to take the vocational track, which was all he was qualified for given his high school record. "I don't really care to be smart, but I know I am smart. And I don't know why it never really mattered to me." He perceived desk jobs as being easier than the work most people have to do, and going back to school might be the only way he will be able to get a desk job. "Working over there in the onions, waking up early in the morning, I didn't like that. No hard labor. Everything is work in life because you can't get it for free, but there's some simple work and hard work, and I want the simple work. It ends up paying more."

"My dad really wants me to study. He knows all the stuff I went through. He hates being told that I'm bright because he knows I ain't doing nothing with it right now. It bothers him. He just says, 'I know he is. Stop reminding me.'" But Enrique was convinced that school never felt right to him and he never felt like he wanted to be there. When he was little he wanted to be an architect because he liked to draw. He gave up that dream: "I saw how hard it was, the way school is and everything. It is pretty hard. And when you want to be something like that you've got to start at a young age. You have to get really good scores on tests and stuff like that." Enrique would like to get a job, but believed that whenever potential employment opportunities came up, the employer would decide not to hire him based on where he lived. "This town has a reputation, so then people think it's like a little drug town. A bunch of Mexicans that don't do nothing. That's what they say."

If he could do things differently, he would have insisted that his parents let him attend a bigger school. "I was a social person and I always wanted to go somewhere big, where there is a different atmosphere and different people. Some kids are made for small schools, but not me." Enrique never expected to graduate from high school: "As a matter of fact, I wasn't really looking forward to it. It wasn't a dream for me and it wasn't that I didn't expect it; I just didn't look forward to it. If it happened, it happened."

He defined a dropout as someone who was different from most people. "The general people, they might just say that this is a druggie or someone that just dropped out. It's a person who has no education at all and is just working at a hard job that pays a cheap price for an hour. They think the person just deserves to drop out, I guess. They think of someone negative, or a bad person. So, then if they think that, then they think that it's good that they dropped out. It's better for the schools." "I wasn't a dropout, I was more of a kicked-out," he laughed. "Not much difference, but I never called myself a dropout. For me, being kicked out and everything, I look for another way to get something. I don't see myself as a dropout because I will still try to go to college. I see a dropout as someone who isn't going to do that." The paradox of high school dropouts discussing the No Child Left Behind Act (2002) was not lost on Enrique. "Yeah, that's what they say, but they never go by the rules."

CHAPTER SIX

Composite Analysis

LATINA/O STUDENTS SEEKING SATISFACTION

As shown in the previous case studies in this book, in the lives of the rural high school dropouts in this study, and from their viewpoint, the reforms of the No Child Left Behind Act (2002) had no positive effect. Youth in this study had all internalized a lack of connection with the work required by schools and a feeling that school personnel did not care for them. The work was seen as boring or useless and not connected with their experience. Students' perception of a lack of caring in schools also contributed to disengagement. Silvia commented pointedly, "I'm just another Mexican. Why would they [teachers and administrators] care about me?" The problem of low expectations for Latino/a youth and acceptance of school dropout in rural schools is consistent with the literature suggesting ubiquitous acquiescence to higher Latino/a dropout rates (Jordan et al., 1999). This chapter first outlines five key themes from our study on the students, their families, and the process of how they came to drop out of school. The next section analyzes what the students experienced in school, and divides the data into six themes. The chapter concludes with our theory of students fighting back and seeking satisfaction by dropping out.

THE STUDENTS, THEIR FAMILIES AND THE PROCESS OF DROPPING OUT OF SCHOOL

This section describes the influences of educators, low self-efficacy, family hardships, lowered asirations, and the lack of family role models on the decision to drop out of school.

*Students were capable of academics, but they did not
connect with teachers and administrators*

Most participants (six out of nine) had passed at least two of the three
NCLB state tests mandated for graduation, so these students could have succeeded academically in school. However, graduation seemed to rest more on
compliance with school policy and procedures, passivity within the classroom, attention to classroom work, and school attendance. Students felt
educators did not care for them, and in turn they did not care for their school
work or educators. They were afraid to ask questions or considered it "weak"
to do so. Because they did not connect with educators to seek the necessary
help, it was hard for them to deliver what the school wanted. "What I did
sometimes was when I really didn't get what they [teachers] said, and stuff
and I knew I was going to flunk, I would just stop doing the work" (Sophia).
"People at school just didn't want me to succeed, so I always felt angry about
it" (Silvia). "I waited and they never helped me" (Maria). Rather than
proactively ask for assistance when they needed it, students avoided educators, just as educators avoided these students and their families.

Students suffered from low self-efficacy with regard to academic success

Low self-efficacy with regard to school success manifested itself during the
interviews. "Maybe they [Whites] are just smarter, I don't know. When
you're Hispanic you have different relationships with your parents when
you're small. Maybe they [Whites] don't have as many problems as we do.
When we were small, like how my mom and dad left each other and it was
just them fighting all the time. I don't know. Maybe they [Whites] just learn
faster or get the stuff better" (Sophia). "They [administrators and teachers]
think the person just deserves to drop out . . . They think of someone negative, or a bad person" (Enrique). The literature also suggested that underper-
formance occurs because stereotypes held by administrators and teachers
encourage negative interpretations that suggest low ability rather than challenges to overcome. Stereotype assignment, a form of racism, adds stress and
self-doubt to the educational experience of students of color (Aronson &
Good, 2002; Nieto, 2004; Steele, 1997).

    Seven out of nine students in this study began school enthusiastically.
The exceptions were Enrique and Victor, who said they had never felt connected with school. Enrique felt "White people don't want us [Hispanics] to
make it." Elementary school, however, was a time of success for most of these
students, and all nine held aspirations for jobs and professions that later were

viewed as impossible to achieve. Over time in school, self-doubt began to be harbored. Somewhere during the middle school years, the idea that school success was not possible for these Latino/a students, and that they in turn did not care for school, became accepted by all of them. "He [the principal] didn't care about us, basically. He didn't see any reason for us to grow up to be something. Our stuff is limited straight out . . . For a while I really tried to do good. I did my best to come to school early and all that stuff. But then I found myself not really caring" (Enrique). "Sometimes I would try to do it [homework], but a lot of the time I didn't understand what they wanted me to do . . . So, I just quit" (Cesar). Similarly, in a study of how stereotypes shape intellectual ability and performance, Steele (1997) explored the question of why students experience the same teacher, textbooks, and classrooms so differently: "Through long exposure to negative stereotypes about their group, members of prejudiced-against groups often internalize the stereotypes, and the resulting sense of inadequacy becomes part of their personality" (p. 617).

Educators were unaware of or ignored family economic hardships

Participants offered views of their decision to drop out of high school that included primarily factors of academic failure, uncaring teachers, hazing, and economic hardship. Experiences beyond their control affected school performance. "I didn't want to quit, but I didn't have anything to do with it. There was nothing for me out of it. I went to work [in the potato harvest] for her [mother] for a month, but I didn't receive anything for that month" (Sophia). Missing a month of school caused Sophia to lose credit for that semester of her junior year.

For Victor circumstances allowed him to live in a friend's car, homeless, for almost two months; he was just 17. Educators did not always know the stresses students were encountering or the family or school circumstances of their students. Not one teacher or administrator knew Victor was living on the streets for two months. "He [the father] went to jail and I didn't have nowhere to go. I couldn't find a job . . . So, I just had to stay wherever I could because my mom didn't want me back" (Victor). Similarly, when the assistant principal was asked about Cesar, he recounted a nice boy who was "quiet, respectful, and a good soccer player." He was not aware that Cesar had been failing courses for some time and as a result had not played soccer in over a year before he dropped out. Educators did not know about, did not seem to care, or did not seem to know how to assist with the stresses students were encountering in classrooms and at home.

Aspirations lowered as students progressed through school

For the youth in this study, feelings of marginalization, disconnection from school, and failure developed during the middle-school years. Enrique wanted to be an architect when he was an elementary school student, but as he grew older he gave up that dream. "I saw how hard it was, the way school is and everything. It is pretty hard. And when you want to be something like that you've got to start at a young age."

"When I was smaller I wanted to be a teacher. I don't think about that now because it's different, and not because I'm a mom. I don't really have anything special that I really want to do. I just want to have a good job. That's all I want to have, and it doesn't matter what it is or what I do. I want a good and easy job" (Sophia). To Sophia, an "easy job" was one that did not entail the back-breaking lifting and physical exertion of lifting heavy milk crates at her present job. To her, a job was preferable to school, where goals seemed unattainable. She added, "It takes a bunch of years to become a teacher, and money to go for a long time to college, or whatever you want to be."

According to one teacher, Victor was his best math student ever. But, as the teacher stated, "in this small town, the kids who do well are involved in sports or other school activities. Those that aren't involved find other things to do, and most of it isn't good." Victor remembered that he wanted to be a doctor when he was younger. "I would always look it up, and it showed that I had to do a lot of college and stuff like that. I wanted to do it real bad. I don't know. It just didn't work out." (Victor). Armando stated, "If I do get my diploma or a GED, around here it won't do me no good." Sadowski's (2003) study found that Latino/a youth from low SES backgrounds sensed that the larger societal barriers of classism and racism severely limited their chances for gaining access to high status careers.

Parents encouraged students to graduate but role models were lacking

"You don't see any Mexicans teaching here. I don't remember not even one teacher being Hispanic in any school I've been in. Not principals either. . . . My dad wanted me to graduate. Even when I was small he would always tell me to graduate" (Sophia). "I went all the way to twelfth grade and I didn't even graduate . . . My sister went with me [to graduation] and she made it into a joke. She said, 'I only made it to tenth grade so don't feel bad.' . . . When I was younger I did really good in school and my mom was always really happy about that because none of my older bothers and sisters had graduated. She always thought I would, so it is kind of hard for her that I didn't finish. She wants me to go to college and get a better job" (Beatriz).

"My parents always wanted me to graduate. They wanted me to go to college, but I never thought I would get that far" (Victor). "They [parents] said things will be easier in your life [with education]. To get a job will be easier" (Victor). "My parents think an education would be a lot more helpful to my life . . . Now all I can work in is factories, plants, dairies" (Armando).

Despite verbal encouragement to stay in school and gain the benefits of a high school diploma, the fact is that most of the parents of participants in this study, and many older adults in these communities, did not graduate from high school themselves. Some of the parents had never attended school at all. This is consistent with the research that shows that there is a racial gap in parental education: 76% of Asian children have parents with at least some college education; 51% of Black children have parents with at least some college education; 35% of Latino children have parents with at least some college education and 73% of White children have parents with at least some college education (National Center for Children in Poverty, 2006).

While education was valued in these students' families, there were additional challenges presented in breaking the pattern of school dropout: "It's kind of hard because we're already thinking, 'Oh, I'm not going to graduate.' That's in our family. Our family didn't graduate. Our moms didn't graduate. Our brothers and sisters didn't graduate. So, it's just normal I guess. I've thought about it. When I was little I knew that my mom only made it to fourth grade here [in the same rural community]. That was because she had to work; back then they had to work. And my brothers and sisters never graduated. I guess when we were little we just saw that and so we tended to do the same things" (Beatriz). Maria expressed her feelings this way: "I feel bad about dropping out, but not that bad because I think they [her parents] understand that school is hard."

WHAT THE STUDENTS EXPERIENCED IN THE SCHOOL ENVIRONMENT

This section depicts the school life of the students. The data is organized by six primary themes that characterize the students' experience.

Text and test-based instruction

The Latino/a dropouts in this study stated a preference for group projects, cooperative-type learning activities, and relevant, "useful" knowledge. However, they felt that their high schools focused on rote, irrelevant textbook learning and testing. They felt that classroom practices had moved away from some of the "fun learning" that had characterized their earlier school-ing. Sophia spoke about the one teacher who still used hands-on, creative methods: "This teacher had a fun way she did it. The other teachers say, 'Here's the book. Do whatever you want.'" Both Victor and Enrique stated, "I was bored." Cesar commented that school learning was not "useful." The use of text and test-based instruction seems to make school less interesting and relevant to Latino/a youth. A shift away from cooperative learning methods that enhance critical thinking made it difficult to meet the learn-ing needs expressed by the Latino/a youth in this study.

English only and "color-blind" policies and practices

School policies and practices were found to be emphasizing assimilation instead of acculturation. Schools were monocultural in a "melting pot" way that the students saw as not valuing their bicultural background, language, and heritage. Not one of the administrators in the high schools was Latina/o and in five schools there were only two Latina/o teachers. The approach to instruction that we found in the schools was based solely on English acquisi-tion. Students were encouraged to essentially "lose Spanish" and "learn Eng-lish." Enrique put it this way: "Here [in school] you gotta be acting White for some teachers." Cristina stated, "Some teachers say that if they [Latino/a stu-dents] can't speak English they shouldn't be in school. I think that is rude. There are some other Mexicans who can speak English that can help them." Armando believed that teachers did not care to even know who he was. These students wanted to fit in—they are Americans—but felt marginalized by a school system that did not celebrate or incorporate their Latino heritage into the learning experience. Their statements are consistent with research that showed that educators neglect and have low expectations for students who do not speak formal English well (Delpit & Dowdy, 2003).

Racism and lack of connection between students and educators

School was a painful experience that included racist incidents for the stu-dents in this study. "She [the teacher] would say things like, 'Are you that dumb that you don't know how to do this? Why do I even waste my time on you guys?'" (Beatriz). In the rural schools in this study Latino/a students felt as if many teachers held low expectations for them and that they were deval-ued as human beings. "Sometimes the teacher won't even bother with you because you're Hispanic" (Silvia). "He [the principal] tried to play an act, you know. Like he was a good principal and he wants me to do good. But in his mind you know he wasn't going to do nothing [to help]!" (Enrique).

These students were not connected with educators and did not seem to know how the system works. Students were not completing work at school, not handing work in, not asking questions when they needed help, and from their points of view, no one seemed to have the expectation that they needed to do these things; no one seemed to care. These students also tended to blame themselves for not succeeding even while describing a school system that expected and accepted their failure.

Educators also blamed Latino/a students for the school not making Annual Yearly Progress (AYP), a reporting requirement of NCLB law. NCLB law states that a school that fails to make AYP in all the student subgroups is labeled a failing school as the first step toward a takeover of the school by the state and possible school closure. Rather than examining the school or their own teaching practices for the Hispanic (HISP) subgroup's failure, educators tended to make the association that failure is the student's fault. "Maybe we should just let them [Hispanic students] go if they want to go" (educator). Silvia argued, "Schools act like they are concerned about their students, but they are more concerned about the grade and the image of their school, which is really sad." Enrique put it this way, "They [the public] think the person just deserves to drop out, I guess. They think of [a dropout as] someone negative, or a bad person. So, then if they think that, then they think that it's good they dropped out. It's better for the schools." The irony of high school dropouts discussing the No Child Left Behind Act (2002) was not lost on Enrique. "Yeah, that's what they [educators and legislators] say, but they never go by the rules." "About No Child Left Behind, I'm proof that there was" (Silvia).

Tracking

Tracking involves dividing students of similar age and ability level into groups for common instruction and usually for focused attention on the skills used to judge student proficiency. Students are well aware of these divisions and the meaning attached to some groups. Tracking is often used to determine which subjects students have to learn, and which careers they may later be qualified to pursue. According to Beatriz, "I was always in the low class, transitions to math or pre-algebra. Fundamentals of Math was for dumb kids and Mexicans" (Beatriz). "I didn't learn anything. I know as much now as I did in 8th grade" (Silvia).

Beatriz described a teacher who taught the Fundamentals of Math class, which was made up of mostly Latino/a students: "She [the teacher] could help us, but she wouldn't. So I just felt like, 'Whatever. I'm not going to do it [the assignment].' She had her favorites, but our class was just a bunch of Mexicans so she hated our class. Everybody would get a 56% on a test and she'd say, 'Why do I even waste my time on you guys? You don't even try.'" (Beatriz). "They [the teachers] judge you before they know you. Schools treat Hispanics different" (Armando). These Latino/a youth felt subjected to institutionalized racism at school at the same time as being a teenager with all the insecurities and fears that arise at that life stage.

Lack of connection between school and home

Neither teachers nor administrators made it a practice to personally contact parents and confer with them when students were failing classes or not attending school. "My dad was gone, and my mom was not really there all the time . . . so we would just not go to school and she wouldn't know" (Beatriz). The students found ways to avoid both attending school and fulfilling school requirements, such as homework. Educators either intentionally or unintentionally allowed these practices to continue. In some cases, students were not even spoken to at the time they left school. One time, the paperwork for transfer to the alternative school was signed and the only person who interacted with the student was the school secretary, who admonished, "OK, be sure to bring your books back." Other students simply disappeared and never came back to school. Only one administrator, the principal at Zaragosa Alternative High School, contacted several students (Armando, Beatriz, and Cristina) after they had dropped out, to ask them to come back to school. However, it seemed to be a case of too little encouragement at a point when their decision had already been made. There was no going back.

Students in this study tended to give up on school when they perceived teachers did not care about them. There was no "fun" for them anymore, such as cooperative learning in class or extracurricular activities such as soccer. There was no connection between home and school. "I was on the dance team in junior high, and I wanted to do it in high school but I didn't even try out because I knew there was no way I could afford it . . . I told them [administrators and teachers] that I was leaving and they just said, 'OK. Just bring all your books back. They didn't even ask why or anything'" (Sophia). Most of the participants in this study made the decision to drop out by themselves without consulting any adult.

Dropping out involved some pushing

Several of the youth in this study could be termed "pushouts." "I wasn't a dropout. I was more of a kicked out" (Enrique). "I just quit trying. I wasn't interested anymore" (Cesar). "I don't really think I wanted to drop out but it happened" (Sophia). Prior to dropping out, Beatriz, Sophia, Armando, Victor, and Enrique were all transferred from the regular high school into alternative schools because of attendance issues and low grades that resulted in a loss of high school credit. The alternative schools were just the final step in the dropout process. For Sophia, becoming a teen mother was the catalyst for moving from high school to alternative school to dropping out. "When I was pregnant I did want to learn, and I still wanted to come and graduate. I still came after I had my baby. Then I came to the alternative school for some time, too. So I don't really think I wanted to drop out, but it just happened." For Silvia, it was the high school principal who actually suggested dropping out of high school as an option for her. This finding is consistent with other studies (Edley & Wald, 2003; DiMaria, 2004; Reeves, 2003; Romo & Falbo, 1996) that suggested a nationwide problem with the "push out" of students from high schools.

SUMMARY STATEMENT:
A THEORY OF STUDENTS SEEKING SATISFACTION

As described in the previous section, six key school practices were evident in the schools that these students had attended: (a) text and test-based instruction, (b) English only and "color-blind" policies and practices, (c) racism, (d) tracking, (e) lack of connection between home and school, and (f) pushing out. These school practices described by students informed our theory of students fighting back against an unresponsive school system and seeking satisfaction. Youth in this study felt that staying in high school and graduating was not a real or viable choice. They did not have good relationships with school teachers, counselors, or administrators. They did not feel that school personnel cared about them. As a result, students tried to fight back, seek personal satisfaction, and reduce their social-psychological pain by leaving.

To preserve their self-esteem, students opted to drop out of school although all of them had the potential for school success. As one example, Silvia said that being Latina meant fighting against an "identity given by society." She spoke of Latino/a friends who had a self-image problem, who did not think they were worth very much, and who would just try to get by. "But not me, I refuse to be a part of it. For me, dropping out wasn't failing. It was succeeding." Given the experiences that these Latino/a youth had in school, it was not a place that contributed to their self-efficacy or feelings of satisfaction.

Friendships in school were valued, but the feeling that teachers didn't like the students; that their home culture and language was devalued; that administrators and teachers wanted them out of school; that the work was "boring" (Enrique), "too hard" (Silvia), "too easy" (Victor), or "not useful" (Cesar) tended to dominate students' feelings about school. "Grades aren't really an issue as long as I'm learning something. If I'm not learning what they're teaching then there isn't much point to having to endure all of the things that come with high school" (Silvia).

Silvia explained it this way, "If I had stayed just to finish high school, my personality, who I was, would have deteriorated . . . I would have had to have been a lower person, and that's not who I am . . . For me dropping out wasn't failing. It was succeeding . . . . You have to do what you have to do, and this is the [solution to the] problem that I chose." Victor stated that he had gained inner strength from his experiences. "It put me through some tough times, but I think it made me stronger. Because, it's like how my dad disciplined me. I'm not a weak person walking around."

These young men and women had a perception that participation in school was detrimental to their sense of self. A sense of pride and self-determination combined to make dropping out an act of resistance to an organizational structure that was not meeting expectations or needs. Silvia felt that she was a stronger person by standing up for herself, even when she felt alone doing it. Enrique had similar sentiments. "I would rather go by what I think over what they [teachers] are trying to get me to think. I trust myself over them . . . It all worked out for me. It really did. I like the way I am. No disappointments" (Enrique). These statements are consistent with research on adolescent identity development and resistance to perceived social class or racism and oppression in school. "Learning what is deliberately taught can be seen as a form of political assent. Not learning can be seen as a form of political resistance" (Erickson, 1993, p. 36).

For most of the dropouts in this study, the act of dropping out was not one they admitted verbally that they regretted. Noncompliance with the dominant norms can lead to acceptance within the home community, even while ensuring failure in school. "Some people will say something and you'll do the opposite. 'I'll prove you wrong.' Do it the hard way. That's what I did. I tell my brother and sister to stay in school and stay out of trouble. They listen, but they're like me" (Victor).

School organization and/or policies clearly contributed to the act of dropping out of school. Cristina used the tactic of acting up in class in order to disguise her lack of connection with teachers and her problem completing assignments. She often wanted to take her work home so that she could get help from her mother. "I wouldn't listen to the teachers and I would do my own thing and take my work home and do it. I would never do it [the assignments] in school. That was the main problem [not doing the work in class]." Maria was often placed in classroom situations for which she was not prepared academically and for which she felt she received little or no help: "I was actually in 10th grade when I was thinking about it [dropping out]. I was thinking that I would like to work in a store or cleaning instead of being in school."

Accepting adult roles as parents or economic providers for the family helped provide satisfaction, pride, and a positive image that the individuals in this study did not get from school. Gaining a sense of independence and fulfilling one's immediate responsibility to the family was evident for these youth. Cesar was able to convince his parents to let him drop out shortly after turning 16, and he immediately found a job. "I always had to ask my parents for this and that, and now I come in with my own money. That's an advantage because I don't have to have the weight of the household all on them. I just keep some and contribute some" (Cesar). Cesar was proud of being able to handle a graveyard shift. "I would hang out with friends or play soccer, but I never missed a single day of work. I always showed up for work on time" (Cesar).

Maria explained, "I'm glad I got a job and went on with that." Armando considered family needs: "Some of the parents don't make that much money to support what they need to live on, and when the potato season comes sometimes their kids have to drop out of school to work for that season. They need to help their family make money to survive. It's not all about dropping out because they want to." Cesar argued, "I was a good worker, and if I go to another dairy the boss will give me a good reference." Sophia described the pride she feels in her parental role, "Right now I have a lot of things to do, and going to work, cleaning, making food, and taking care of my son is one of the best things." Beatriz also stated, "I'm young, but I take very good care of my kids. They have everything they need. That's something to be proud of. They are real happy kids."

Young men can also find parenthood rewarding. Armando found fulfillment in the relationship with his son, and hoped he would be a good father to him. "I like to spend time with my son the most. When I'm with him, that's the best I can do" (Armando). Halle & LeMenestrel (1999) found that economic conditions may lead fathers to seek alternative ways to be involved with their children, as Armando did when he moved back in with his parents in order to have enough money to provide child support for his son.

Being able to contribute monetarily to the family was important for these youth who exhibited a strong sense of family loyalty, to *mi familia*. "I just do whatever I can because I feel sorry for them [his brothers] because my dad's not there. The refrigerator is empty, and their clothes are from last year. As soon as I get a job I'm going to buy both my brothers some clothes" (Victor). "It would be kind of hard to move away [to seek work] because of how my dad is [disabled]. He's not doing well. My mom, she needs help on some of the bills. I don't want to leave her out there like that" (Armando).

These Latino/a youth also believed that education was not enough to succeed. Study participants remarked that graduating from high school did not necessarily guarantee a successful career. "My sister was all about school, and so was my brother . . . They liked school work" (Cesar). For Cesar, the fact that both siblings, despite graduating from high school, had only been able to acquire employment as laborers confirmed the notion that graduating may not provide success. "Not graduating wasn't a good thing, because it's really hard to get hired and even harder in the winter. If you graduate it's a little bit better, but it's still really hard when there are no jobs" (Sophia). "To tell you the truth, if I do get my diploma or GED, around here it won't do me no good" (Armando). All four of the boys in this study and one of the girls were currently unemployed although they were working in their own homes by cleaning, helping with younger siblings, driving mothers around town, or taking care of their own children, a sick dad or grandmother. Four of the girls in this study worked in minimum wage jobs, lifting milk crates, sorting onions, packing cherries, waiting tables, babysitting, cleaning or dishwashing. Silvia held three part-time jobs to make ends meet.

Latino/a youth felt overwhelmed by processes both in school and in their families that were out of their control. "I know my parents always cared, but they didn't go to school. They were struggling, too, and they couldn't pay too much attention and help us with our homework because they were always busy or something" (Victor). Teachers, counselors, and administrators, from the students' perspectives, did nothing to take into account or attend to students' personal problems. Instead, students felt that educators disliked them. These students had a few educators throughout their school careers who had cared, but they needed a school-wide culturally responsive system based on caring, with high expectations for academic success, inclusion in essential extracurricular activities, and connections with families.

Enrique stated, "Maybe if he [the school principal] would have connected with me, I obviously would have done something better and it would have benefited him as a principal. But that would have been hard and he wanted it easy. He saw us as a waste of time." Both sides seemed to blame the other: educators saw the students as having an "attitude" problem, and students saw the educators as "not caring." Cristina stated, "I don't think most people are even bothered by people who drop out because there are a lot of kids who drop out around here." School personnel are in a position to be a lifeline for students with regard to school success, but for the students in this study, they were not. The students developed feelings of not being wanted at school or liked by school personnel and they fought back and sought satisfaction by dropping out of school.

SUMMARY

These Latino students experienced a school environment that did not keep them busy, motivated, and engaged, and that marginalized them. Schooling was something done to them rather than something done by and for them. All in all, the requirements of the No Child Left Behind Act of 2001 (2002) meant little to these youth growing up poor and rural, and who felt unsupported in school. School was an experience marked by teachers who were perceived as not caring and who held low expectations for them, work that was dry and removed from their experience, and a school climate and culture that devalued them as students and as individuals.

NCLB includes parent and family involvement as a measure of school success, yet these students and their families did not experience any enhanced efforts of the schools to connect with families or to ensure that students stayed in school. Indeed, as we show in this book, educators were unaware of basic needs, essential to learning, such as the fact that Victor was living out of a friend's car for two months. In addition, when students left school, administrators and teachers did not consult with students or their families, but routinely signed the paperwork for transfer to the alternative school (which kept these students in school for only several more weeks or months). At times they were oblivious to the fact that students had, in fact, dropped out of high school. One administrator described how soccer keeps kids in school, naming one of our dropouts as an example. The administrator expressed surprise when told by us that the student had dropped out the previous year.

Ogbu (1987) described how failing to achieve academically can be interpreted by some students of color as an accomplishment, in a defiant stance to the dominant culture. Our findings differed in that the students stated that their school failure was not an accomplishment. The students did not see dropping out as an accomplishment at all. They were aware that their own parents and society in general often views dropping out of school as a failure. However, schooling was not rewarding for these students and they subsequently sought satisfaction through other arenas (e.g., parenthood, employment opportunities, drug and risk-taking behaviors). They had once wanted to be a doctor, lawyer, teacher, architect, but their chances for accomplishing these dreams were diminished. However, they saw themselves as "good people" and had enough self-respect to take themselves out of the school environment that was treating them as "bad people." If they had been mentored to experience success in school through caring relationships with teachers, sports or extracurricular activities, and appreciation of their cultural heritage, this may have been enough to keep students in school. The case studies are particularly poignant because all the students appeared to be capable of school success as indicated by prior school success, and passing grades on all or sections of the ISAT. The decision to drop out was made in all cases without consultation with an educator, although all the schools had school counselors and administrators on staff.

The rural schools and communities in our study upheld a class-based society. It is our conclusion from this study that by middle school, students became conscious of classism and racism in their rural settings, which contributed to school disengagement. These students, under pressure to look good for their peers, could not keep up the pretense that everything was OK. They were hurting economically and academically and, in the face of this hurt, at least they could try to be popular with peers and let dreams of school success go. Others took jobs when they became available and focused on helping out at home and buying the things that most kids want.

We have emphasized the point throughout the book that Latina/o students are typically blamed for their own failure in school, and the students frequently blamed themselves as well. "I was a troublemaker," said Armando. "I wouldn't listen," argued Cesar. "Maybe I expected too much," stated Sophia. Blaming the students, the families, or society without examining what can be done in schools is not helpful and contributes to the severe dropout problem today. Culturally responsive leadership is a way to address the problem and includes loving respect or caring, *con cariño,* which is in the subtitle of Chapter 1 and explained more fully in Chapter 7. The following words of Silvia point to the need for culturally responsive leadership that is grounded in educators establishing a caring, personal connection with their students. She shows how schools are, in some cases, trying to hide the truth, blocking the sun out with a finger.

High school.
If you can go in class and feel safe and secure
Because you have a one-on-one relationship with the teacher,
That's probably enough to keep you going through school.
High school.
There's only what you look at.
And you think it's real because that's what they give you to look at.
So, your principal gives you the image of what your school is,
Because that's what he wants you to see.
If he sees the flaws, everyone sees the flaws.
He doesn't want them to see, so he doesn't admit it.

CHAPTER SEVEN

A Leadership Plan for Culturally Responsive Schools

SCHOOLING CON CARIÑO

We show in this book many of the daily policies and practices in rural schools that contributed to Latino/a students' lack of success and eventual drop out of school. We found low expectations for student success, tracking programs with overrepresentation of Latino/a students, "color-blind" curriculum and pedagogy, a lack of diverse staff, and no direct contact with parents when students skipped school or had failing grades. Educators blamed students in subgroups for a school's failure status, and students were discouraged from speaking Spanish at school. Students reported harassment and name-calling and felt neglected or even disliked by teachers. We are not blaming the students, their families, administrators, or teachers; instead, we want to build on the commitment that educators have to see all students succeed. The perspective of the students is helpful in ensuring that school policies and practices are positive and welcoming to Latina/o students to enhance their experiences in school and to encourage school success.

The National Education Association (2006c) has recently proposed 12 helpful action steps for dropout prevention:

1. Mandate high school graduation or equivalency as compulsory for everyone below the age of 21.
2. Establish high school graduation centers for students 19–21 years old.
3. Make sure students receive individualized attention.
4. Expand students' graduation options.

107

5. Increase career education and workforce readiness programs in schools.
6. Act early so students do not drop out.
7. Involve families in students' learning at school and at home.
8. Monitor students' academic progress in school.
9. Monitor, accurately report, and work to reduce dropout rates by gathering accurate data for key student groups (such as racial, ethnic, and economic).
10. Involve the entire community in dropout prevention.
11. Make sure educators have the training and resources they need to prevent students from dropping out.
12. Make high school graduation a federal priority with funds allocated by Congress.

We agree with the NEA recommendations, but they are brief and generalized. In this book we provide a comprehensive plan with specific strategies focused on providing educators with the training and resources needed to reshape the currently alienating "color-blind" school environment. Our plan for culturally responsive schools is based on students' experiences and is a logical step for administrators, teachers, and counselors to enhance the possibilities of student retention and success. We did not want to conduct a study that simply showed the problem but offered no solutions. We were careful to derive this leadership plan from the experiences of the students and not simply impose our own solutions. Where appropriate we use the students' words and experiences to illustrate each component of the plan.

This chapter is written for school superintendents, principals, teachers, counselors, and the university faculty who work with them. It provides a guide for leaders to develop and implement their own culturally responsive leadership plan. Stakeholders should be invited to the table to participate in the creation of a plan tailored to each unique school or school district. A culturally responsive leadership plan is a strategic plan for a school or school district that specifically focuses on creating a school environment where (a) staff and students can develop multicultural knowledge, skills, and dispositions; (b) principals work to ensure that test scores are equitable across different ethnic and cultural groups and that all student groups are succeeding, and (c) families and communities are included in the educational process. (See Riehl, (2000) for a literature review of tasks that multicultural leaders need to serve culturally diverse schools.)

All schools have goals and a school improvement plan of some kind and all districts have a strategic plan. However, not all these plans include cultural responsiveness as an articulated goal that is reinforced in all policies and practices. Our culturally responsive leadership plan has the goal of enhancing educational success for Latino/a students and enriching the education of all students through an engaging and stimulating multicultural and culturally relevant education.

Our plan contains 10 action items or objectives, with strategies included for each item. The acronym for the plan is RESPONSIVE. R stands for the objective of garnering resources and revising the plan for each unique setting; E is for establishing culturally responsive (not "color-blind") missions, policies, and practices; S is for including the Spanish language; P is for providing a culturally responsive curriculum, instruction, and assessment; O is for offering care that is personalized with high expectations for academic success; N is for saying no to racism and for anti-racism professional development; S is for staffing diversified employees; I is for implementing heterogeneous classes with differentiated instruction; V is for varying counseling roles; and E is for valuing every parent. Savvy teachers, counselors, or administrators can select an item or implement several intervention strategies and continually assess their progress. In some schools it may be an informal leader—an individual teacher—not the principal at all, who has the leadership abilities to create a culturally responsive school. To evaluate success, collect data before, during, and after implementation of the plan. Figure 1 represents the plan in a simple diagram.

FIGURE 1. CULTURALLY RESPONSIVE LEADERSHIP PLAN
USING THE ACRONYM RESPONSIVE

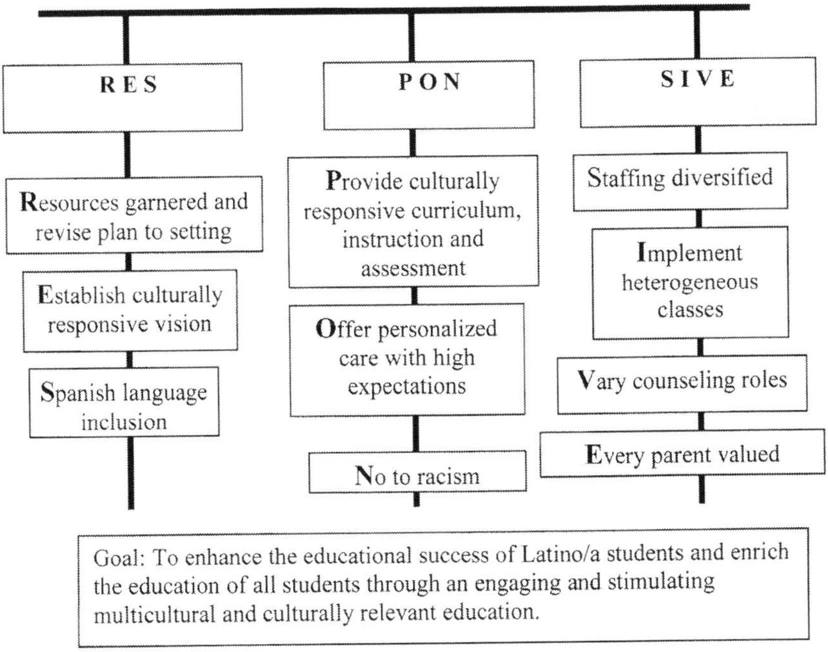

Goal: To enhance the educational success of Latino/a students and enrich the education of all students through an engaging and stimulating multicultural and culturally relevant education.

A LEADERSHIP PLAN FOR CULTURALLY RESPONSIVE SCHOOLS

Resources garnered, revise plan to unique setting

ACTION ITEM #1

Some of the action items in this chapter require no additional funding; others do. Teachers do not have a budget, but they can work with their administrators to ensure that funds are set aside to accomplish the goal of creating culturally responsive classrooms and schools. We pay for what we value. If we value the success of all students, we need to demonstrate that desire with resources. Teachers and administrators can also seek government, foundation, and community support. Grant writing takes time, and time is in short supply for educators. However, many government and private foundations and community organizations have a vested interest in seeing Latino/a students succeed in school and the time may be well spent by seeking additional resources from these places. To begin, educators can identify each action item that they want to accomplish in their school and then seek partners in sponsors and grants to make these goals possible. After showing sponsors and funding agencies the benefits of what will be accomplished, additional resources will likely be forthcoming.

Establish culturally responsive, not "color-blind" mission, policies, and practices

ACTION ITEM #2

Principals and teachers informed us throughout this study: "I don't see color. I teach children." They are trying to be impartial and "color blind." Yet in not seeing color or students' languages, cultures, and heritage, they are denying their students the opportunity to share who they are with them and their peers. Armando felt, for instance, that teachers did not care to even know who he was. The heritage, cultures, and languages of diverse students can provide rich learning opportunities in the classroom. Students may also lose a natural commitment to learning when they are not appreciated and valued in school. Knowledge is built on prior experience and if the school does not validate the students' prior experience, their learning potential and motivation may be diminished. (For more on the fallacy of a "color-blind" approach, see Anderson, 2006; L. Bell, 2002; Delpit, 1995; Frankenberg, 1993; S. Marx, 2004; Ovando, 2006; Thompson, 1998; Williams, 1997.)

Other educators seemed to see color only in terms of the negative stereotypes that may have been attributed to a group. A teacher in this study stated that "most of the teachers in the school" were "afraid" of Enrique. Where was this coming from if not from a fear of people not known or stereotypes of Latino/a gang members? The language of fear only encourages a lack of connection between students, staff, teachers, and administrators. The result can be a disconnection for students of color from what Delpit (1995) referred to as "alienating environments" (p. 5).

A school or school district can express the importance of the diverse families that schools serve by incorporating diversity and multiculturalism into the school mission and goals. For example, a goal can be "to create a caring school climate and culture that values diversity and multicultural- ism." Administrators can then use statements such as this one to assess school effectiveness through, for example, curriculum, instruction, and assessment of student outcomes. If diversity and building respect in our eth- nically and culturally diverse society is valued, then it should be reflected in a written expectation that is reinforced by school leaders in their everyday verbal communications and in the way they walk their talk.

District and school policies and practices also need to be examined for equity and fairness. For instance, in one district a letter sent to all parents explained that their children's school had not met Adequate Yearly Progress (AYP) goals as mandated by the NCLB Act. The parents were then informed that they had the right to move their children to a higher per- forming school, if there was one to move to. The letter also stated that the reason the district did not meet AYP goals was because of "Hispanic reading and math scores." While the information was factual, the underlying tone of the communication was to blame Latino/a students for their inability to per- form as well as White students. Communication such as this can divide com- munities and erode trust with families.

Our study also found that Latino/a youth left school because organiza- tions did not give them reasons to stay. Simple policy changes, such as the following, would be helpful in the rural schools we studied were:

- Establish intercultural organizations and groups. Intercultural education aims at developing a school climate and culture of community, trust, personal involvement, responsibility, and respect in our ethnically and culturally diverse society (Leeman, 2003).
- Remove pay-to-play policies for sports and extracurricular activ- ities, or find ways of providing for students who cannot afford to pay.
- Remove policy stating that participation in extracurricular activities is dependent on good grades.
- Provide school yearbooks free of charge. Funds could be obtained from community service organizations, such as the Lions Club, and community members.

- Revise attendance policies to be relevant for today's students. One of the alternative schools had a strict "three days absence and you're out" policy, which did not take into account the adult lives of these students, three of whom were teen parents.
- De-track school classes and replace them with heterogeneous classes using differentiated instruction.
- Revise the zero-tolerance expulsion policy to ensure it is used for the specific infractions for which it was initially created: drug and weapon possession in school. Unfortunately, this policy seems to have been expanded to enable school officials to push out those they view as the "lesser kids," chronic truants, "troublemakers," or disruptors that are bothersome but not dangerous. A study by Verdugo (2002) showed that the zero-tolerance policy was disproportionately used against poor students, Latinos, and African Americans for trivial offenses. For a set of recommendations for developing a sound zero-tolerance policy, see Verdugo 2002.
- Establish academic support systems for struggling students, for example, a mentoring program. Sophia stated, "I wouldn't ask for help because I didn't know anyone in the class . . . and I thought the teacher wouldn't help me so I just didn't ask." Once students have been identified as being at risk of educational failure, school administrators could assign mentors to lead them through the path of academic success. Ensure that at least some of the mentors are themselves Latino/a.
- Hold grade-level meetings. Grade-level meetings held from one to three times per week are a way to share effective strategies, coordinate and align the curriculum across the grade level, and plan common curriculum themes. All general education, ELL, ESL, PEP, and special education teachers could participate. The goal is to create a unified school where all students are challenged, held to high standards, and exposed to a common, and engaging, curriculum.
- Examine all areas for the equality of their policies (e.g., student leadership, athletics, absenteeism due to national or international travel).

An explanation of how these recommendations connect with the research base and our findings follows.

Some of the students in our study were involved in extracurricular activities in junior high school (e.g., basketball, dance, soccer) and they were good at these activities. However, economic factors or school policies concerning low grades prevented their participation in high school. Success in extracurricular activities may help improve school grades. The literature showed a consistent relationship between engaging in extracurricular activities and staying in school. Kaufman (2001), in his work with the *High School and Beyond* data, found that fewer students who participated in sports and other extracurricular activities dropped out of high school. Janosz, LeBlanc, Boulerice, and Tremblay (1997), in a study of 791 adolescents, found that dropout prevention programs are most effective when they target school commitment and school achievement. School commitment is built upon measures, such as extracurricular activities and caring adult contacts, that encourage students to stay in school.

Extracurricular activities connect the high school student to the school, whether these activities are clubs or sports. Although school achievement is important for dropout prevention, caution must be given not to attach punitive measures to activities that cultivate school commitment: "Requiring a decent grade-point-average to participate in extracurricular activities may increase the proportion of students who drop out" (Dornbusch & Kaufman, 2001, p. 84). Aware teachers and counselors, with the support of their administrators, must work to intervene. They can revise extracurricular policies and in so doing provide the necessary encouragement for student success.

All school policies should be examined with sensitivity to issues that marginalize Latinos or other populations. A White female student related an incident that occurred during her first year in a rural school. The teen entered seventh grade after attending a local private school through sixth grade. She decided she wanted to run for seventh-grade class secretary, but was subsequently informed that she was ineligible because she hadn't attended a public school in the district the year before. When her parents met with administrators about this school policy, they were told it was in place to keep "the migrant kids" from running for office. "We only want the best kids to run," the parents were told. However, this girl's parents were offended by the racism in the school and worked to change the policy. No one had ever questioned the policy before, and no one knew how long it had been in place.

Gay (2000) outlined the dilemmas Latino families face when making the decision to move to the United States. Imagine coming to the United States from Mexico to escape poverty and to make a better life. You have left the support of your extended family. The schooling your children had in Mexico was intermittent, and perhaps unaffordable. Now that you are here, you must move often or change jobs frequently. Your children are not happy at school and don't feel welcome.

They have to adjust to a new culture, language, style of living, and educational system. This geographic, cultural, and psycho-emotional uprootedness can cause stress, anxiety, feelings of vulnerability, loneliness, isolation, and insecurity. All of these conditions have negative affects on school achievement. (Gay, 2000, p. 17)

Add to this the confusion you must feel when you are admonished by school authorities not to take your children out of school beyond the week or so provided at Christmas time. You can't go back to Mexico during the summer months when the children are not in school because that is the time when you will be working to feed and clothe the family. Now you are told you can't take your children to visit your family in the winter because they will miss too much school and lose credit. If this were an upper-middle-class family taking the children to Europe would school accommodations be provided? Would this trip be viewed as an enriching educational travel experience? Just thinking about these two similar scenarios helps us to see some ways our school policies and practices are viewed as uncaring.

Spanish language inclusion and language-sensitive programs offered

ACTION ITEM #3
In schools with a significant population of Latino students, staff can be encouraged from the top levels of administration to make a commitment to learn Spanish in order to reach out and communicate with those Latino parents for whom Spanish is their home language. Although the goal is to have all students fluent and competent in English, the Spanish language can be a bridge to connect families with schools. Research shows that more than half of Latino/a students speak mostly English at home; however, 25% percent of all Latino/a students in the United States speak mostly Spanish at home (Llagas, 2003, p. T2). In the following ways, communication between families and schools can be enhanced:

- Written communication can be provided in Spanish, for example, letters concerning grades or attendance.
- Bulletin boards can be displayed in English and Spanish, and bilingual pamphlets can be placed in the school lobby.
- Consider the benefits of second language opportunities and discuss the issue with parents. All students would benefit from learning a second or third language, not just Latino students. In today's global economy, dual-immersion English/Spanish classes may be a good model for some schools with an even proportion

of both native English and native Spanish speakers. In two-way bilingual education (TWBE) practices, native English-speaking students are mixed with native Spanish speakers to create a balanced class, and instruction is provided in both languages. Two-way bilingual education is currently not implemented in any public school in Idaho, according to the definition provided by the Center for Applied Linguistics (2005). Instead of bilingual education, the Sheltered Instruction Observation Protocol (SIOP) model is currently popular in California, Oregon, Washington, and Idaho. This model offers a sheltered English lesson planning and implementation approach for English language learners. The main feature of SIOP is its attention to both content and language objectives for every lesson. The approach consists of eight components and 30 features that are explained in the book, *Making Content Comprehensible for English Learners: The SIOP Model* (Echevarria, Vogt, & Short, 2004). The eight components are Lesson Preparation, Building Background, Comprehensible Input, Strategies, Interaction, Practice/Application, Lesson Delivery, and Review/Assessment.

The important point is not the particular approach or model that is endorsed or whether second languages are taught, but that administrators are connecting with parents, listening to their needs, and creating better learning opportunities for immigrants students learning a second language. Latino/a parents may not want bilingual education for their children. They may want English-only instruction. In the state of Idaho all the high-stakes tests (e.g., the Idaho Reading Indicator for grades 1–3) are given in English, so parents may want every advantage their children can receive to do well on the tests, including classroom instruction in English.

Even if a school does decide to provide instruction in English only, this does not mean that the Spanish language has no place inside the school. In some schools, enrolling in a second-language course would be seen as a positive educational opportunity. This was not the case in the rural schools we studied. Some of the youth described teachers who prohibited Spanish speaking in core classes because the educator did not speak Spanish and did not trust that students were on-task. This not only led to a negative climate where students felt devalued, but also prevented students from discussing difficult content knowledge in their "thinking language." Imagine yourself trying to explain or understand a physics concept in a language in which you are not competent. Imagine then being tested in that "foreign" language. How would that feel? What would your understanding of physics be?

Learning the language of Latino/a students, even in a rudimentary way, is another overt sign to students that teachers care. This may sound daunting, but students who come to school without an English base are struggling too. Second-language learners have even more obstacles to success than English-speaking Latinos. Inability to communicate with a student is frustrating; however, the teacher must realize that it is frustrating for the student as well. If the teacher reaches out and makes connections, the process will be easier for both parties.

Teachers do not have to be fluent in Spanish to begin to build positive relations with students, but they do have to make some effort to learn their students' home language. Carolyn puts it this way: "My attempts at speaking in Spanish with my students have given them all sorts of delightful stories to share. I have vivid memories of the day I was trying to describe in Spanish the antics of my dog. I called her *perra* because, of course I knew that *perro* meant dog and my dog is a girl and so I wanted to use the feminine form of the word. I will leave it to you and your Spanish-English dictionary to figure out what I said. My students teased me about it, lovingly, for the rest of the year. My students and I had a caring relationship based on my attempts to include them in the learning process."

Provide culturally responsive curriculum, instruction, and assessment

ACTION ITEM #4

School instruction contains within it hidden values that students are expected to learn. School curriculum is connected with the larger school climate and culture. In an earlier study of the cultures of two private schools, Mary found that the elite college-preparatory school was sending a message through its curriculum of individual competitiveness coupled with a moral message of servant leadership. The other school, a Waldorf or Rudolf Steiner school, through its arts-based and storytelling curriculum and instruction, was emphasizing connection with nature and one another (Henry, 1993). In our public schools, attention also needs to be given to the hidden curriculum or messages that are being sent to students through the curriculum that is selected and the way it is delivered. If the diverse students in our public schools do not see themselves well represented in the curriculum, instruction, and staff they can erroneously conclude that schooling is not for them.

Counselors, teachers, and administrators who themselves are Latino/a or willing to learn about Latino/a culture, history, and contributions become better educators for Latina/o students because they can share knowledge and experiences. Culturally knowledgeable teachers are able to offer a more comprehensive curriculum to all students. One principal argued that his school had adopted a multicultural curriculum and pedagogy a long time ago. Yet in his own school, as just one example, in the fourth-grade Idaho history text, *A Rendezvous With Idaho History* (Dutton & Humphries, 1994), all the people in the chapter entitled "Famous People," were White. Teachers who use this text need to be culturally responsive in their pedagogy by explaining to the class that at the time this recent history was being created in Idaho, the White privilege of that time meant that the achievements of White people were the only ones recorded. Teachers need to stress that textbooks are written from the point of view of the times and the writer. In this way, critical thinking skills would be developed in the students. Teachers could demonstrate that achievements can be heroic in everyday existence, and not just in the publicly recognized realm. The Latino/a farm worker, Chinese immigrant railroad worker, Japanese immigrant farmers, parents of all ethnicities, or the Black cowboy have all contributed as much to Idaho's development and historical legacy as the White males featured in the text.

The students in this study referred to themselves as "just another Mexican" instead of having pride and a feeling of inclusion in the school curriculum. Students tended to blame themselves for their lack of success in school. "Maybe White students are just smarter," said Sophia. They are not smarter, but they are more privileged, as things currently stand in the rural schools we studied. Education needs to be redefined, not as a White privilege, but for everyone. Education also needs to be projected as a very cool thing to do. Success in school should not mean that one takes a risk of becoming less popular or viewed as a White nerd. Multiculturalism needs to be celebrated every day if it is to be effective. Latino/a students will begin to feel valued and incorporated and all students will be better educated. All students need to be knowledgeable and able to communicate with and appreciate people from all backgrounds and cultures. The great strength of the United States is its unique ability to create a nation from the many cultures, backgrounds, heritages, and languages that enrich its people. We are selling ourselves short if we do not teach all our students to appreciate and value all our diverse people in a caring community of learners.

Principals can take an instructional leadership role and ensure that teachers add multicultural and culturally relevant pictures on the classroom walls, books in the library, and examples in lessons that show a variety of people being heroic every day. Students not only like to see themselves represented in the curriculum, but also learn at a faster rate and are more engaged in learning when they believe that the curriculum relates to them. A. Ferguson (2001) showed that educators who are ethnocentric, viewing their students as "culturally disadvantaged" simply because of their ethnicity, have a devastating effect on students' willingness to learn. Principals who are culturally responsive leaders have high expectations for academic success.

They spend time in classrooms and ensure that teachers are including culturally relevant knowledge in the curriculum and in their instruction. Evaluation of teachers (and principals) would include multicultural proficiency as a dimension of evaluation.

Educators who are culturally responsive have high expectations for the academic success of all students regardless of their socioeconomic, linguistic, or cultural background. In the classroom, these educators ensure that library and instructional materials portray characters in a realistic way, and not in a sexist, racist, or stereotypical manner (Nieto, 2004, pp. 383–384). Teachers who are sensitive to the lives of Latino/a, Asian American, American Indian, African American, and White youth (Irish American, Italian American, Bosnian, and so on) and the differences each student brings into the classroom will become knowledgeable about different learning styles. Research suggests that school instructional environments that are caring, nurturing, and respectful of students and their cultures are also able to boost achievement (Lockwood & Secada, 1999). School achievement for all will likely occur when attention is paid to developing a culture of caring for each student as an individual, as a member of different cultural groups, and as a member of the school family.

Part of paying attention is learning about the cultures of Latina/o students. Be aware that there are many different groups that fall under the Latina/o umbrella. In the schools in which we were involved, the students were most often of Mexican heritage, so the ideas we present here are with them in mind. Some of the following recommendations may be applicable to other Latina/o groups in the United States as well (e.g., Puerto Rican, Cuban, or Guyanese). Educators should constantly be aware not to overgeneralize or stereotype, but to learn from individual students and their families. At the same time, there are Latina/o cultural values that all educators could be aware of even while knowing that they do not apply in all cases.

Elements of a culturally responsive curriculum could include the following:

- Curriculum content needs to include the achievements of people from all cultures. For instance, literature, history, social studies, and business courses could include studies of famous Latinos, such as Cesar Chavez (1927–93, activist for rights of Hispanic farm workers), Alberto Gonzales (attorney general in the George W. Bush administration, 2006), Bill Richardson (governor of New Mexico), Joan Baez (folk singer), Cruz Bustamante (politician), Sandra Cisceros (writer), Alex Rodriguez (baseball player), Richard Rodriguez (Pulitzer prize–winning author), Carlos Santana (rock-and-roll musician), Cheech

Marin (entertainer), Eduardo Castro-Wright (CEO of Walmart USA) and Lydia Villa-Komaroff (scientist). The text *100 Hispanic Americans Who Changed History* (Laezman, 2005) contains many examples of noteworthy achievements of Latina/os for teachers to include. The same series includes titles that present the achievements of other Americans, such as Native Americans and African Americans, who also have traditionally been neglected in school curriculum and instruction. A caution is in order here. Given the history of racism in the United States, studying historical events or figures can sometimes be depressing for students of color. Imagine how you would feel if a book presented your kinship group as traumatized (e.g., slavery, assassination of Dr. Martin Luther King, Jr.) and discriminated against (e.g., unequal and segregated schools). There is nothing wrong with learning from the past, but the past needs to be presented sensitively and in a manner that includes historical context. Ensure that positive and successful *contemporary* role models who are persons of color are included frequently in the curriculum and instruction.

- To engage students in science and math education, problems should be drawn from fields that relate to the life experiences of Latina/os and address issues that encompass practical and social aspects of science and math (Tobias, 1990). The students in our study were refusing to learn in classes that were, in their own words, "for dumb kids and Mexicans" (Beatriz); these classes emphasized decontextualized repetitive drills and fundamental computations. If the excitement of learning can be kindled, students will likely respond by learning.

- Cooperative learning is supported by both theory and research as an effective instructional model, especially for Latino/a youth, as are explicit strategies that develop metacognitive skills. According to research, Latino/a students prefer conformity, peer-oriented learning, kinesthetic instructional strategies [involving movement and physical activity in learning], a high degree of structure, and variety, as opposed to routines (Griggs & Dunn, 1996). Traditionally, for Latinos, "learning takes place verbally, through storytelling, apprenticeship, and experiences . . . schools tend to be competitive, whereas the Hispanic culture is cooperative" (Wells, 1999, p. 8).

- Assigning older students as mentors can help build on individual strengths of Latina/o students and give them opportunities to share their experiences. Mentors can also help keep students engaged in the learning process (Menchaca & Ruiz-Escalante, 1995).

- It is imperative that possible disengagement from school be identified at an early age and prevented by maintaining high expectations for academic success and ensuring that children are successful in school.
- All students—gifted, average, English Language Learners (ELL), and Potentially English Proficient (PEP) learners—need an enriched and supportive environment. (We prefer Gonzales's (2002, p. 13) term Potentially English Proficient to Limited English Proficient, the term used in federal guidelines, because it respects the students' ability to learn and does not label them with a deficiency.)
- Tests should be created that tap into higher-level thinking skills and allow students to show what they know and can do in a variety of formats and contexts. Silvia pointedly asked, "Why can't we write what we know or make a presentation? That would show more than a test, or more than an A, B, or C answer. Couldn't we show what we can do rather than just writing on the tests?" Although tests provide valuable information for instruction, care should be taken when using them to make high-stakes decisions (Clarke, Abrams, & Madaus, 2001, p. 224).
- Students can compose and be creative in Spanish, through poetry, prose, or songs. Initially, students should be allowed to write for the sake of writing. A playwright, poet, or musician might just evolve. Teachers can expose students to different genres in communication, authors, and writings such as Sandra Cisneros's story of a Latino (Puerto Rican) barrio in Chicago, entitled *House on Mango Street* (1984); Lorie Carlson's collections of poems written by Latino/as growing up in the United States, *Cool Salsa* (1994) and *Red Hot Salsa* (2005); Federico Garcia Lorca's *Bodas de Sangre* (*Blood Wedding*) (2001); and Rudolfo Anaya's story of a Mexican American boy growing up in New Mexico in the period of Workd War II, *Bless Me Ultima* (1995).
- Cultural study and experiences can be added that include people, history, foods, festivals, dances, costumes, attire, literature, art, music, games, and cultural events from the students' own experiences in the United States:
  - *Quinceañeras* (Sweet 15). A celebration marking the transition from childhood to womanhood.

- *Cinco de mayo* (Fifth of May). A celebration in the United States of the victory of Mexican forces over the French in 1862. Celebration includes fiesta, dancing, food, and music (Tiedt & Tiedt, 2005, p. 281).
- *El dia de los muertos* (Day of the Dead). A celebration on November 2 with special sweets to feed the spirits of ancestors, and with masks and skeletons to scare spirits away (Tiedt & Tiedt, 2005, p. 256). At Yolanda's school, students celebrated the day in October by dressing up as skeletons, witches, ghosts, and goblins. Students cooked *el pan muerto* (bread), which is often shaped into skulls or bones, and *pasole* (shredded pork with hominy beans) for the teachers. The event brought a sense of community and participation for all.
- Students can share holidays, cultures, and traditions they have brought to the United States from other countries, such as Mexico, Spain, Peru, and other South American countries. For example, September 16, *El Dia de Independencia* (Mexican Independence Day) can be celebrated. Also, Mexican heritage and culture can be studied not just during National Hispanic Heritage month from September 15 to October 15, but throughout the year.
- The following examples of Latino/a values and cultural terms should be understood by teachers and possibly incorporated into curriculum and instruction:
  - *La Familia* (the family). One of the most cohesive forces of the Latino community is caring, cooperation, and contribution to *la familia*. Siblings are expected to support and help each other (Cooper, Denner, & Lopez, 1999). However, the cohesive force of the family is not true for every Latino family (Carrasquillo, 1994). Educators do need to understand the importance of family, however, in order to mentor and work with students. Educators can encourage the idea that it is possible to value familial interdependence without subverting personal educational success goals, because individual success can be materially beneficial to the family and the community (California Tomorrow, 2002).
  - *Respeto* (respect). Respect of elders is a key part of Latino culture. Adults are the bearers of wisdom, not children, and parents' positions and knowledge is to be highly valued. Trumbull, Rothstein-Fisch, Greenfield, & Quiroz (2001) suggested that school assignments could honor this value by having students interview elders and report on important

cultural stories, beliefs, or experiences, thus enhancing multi-cultural awareness and understanding. Parents may be honored to visit with a class and share cultural artifacts, crafts, music, dance, stories, or ideas if they know that the wisdom and knowledge that they share is greatly appreciated (Nieto, 2004; Cooper et al., 1999; D'Emilio, 2002; Dorfman & Fisher, 2002). In our study we also found that the parents valued education highly and respected educators, but the Latino/a students needed advocates in school. For example, Silvia's IEPs were not met in high school; Cristina was no longer involved in school activities; Maria was struggling with homework until 12:00 at night; Beatriz wanted to be on the dance team in high school but knew there was no way she could afford it. Educators need to understand that it may not be possible for parents to be engaged in the ways that they envisage, and they need to reach out to these students and their families and advocate for their students' success. When the students are experiencing success in school the communication may be easier to establish: no one wants to hear bad news, particularly if the bad news is accompanied by blaming. Lack of communication between school and home occurred in all the cases of the dropouts in this study. Educators have a responsibility in these cases to serve as advocates for the students.

- *Machismo*. Within Latino/a culture, there is a strong commitment to respect the tradition of chivalry, but not male dominance. Latinas, as in other ethnic groups, are often the head of the household as a single parent.
- *La Raza* (race and culture). Pride in the Latino heritage and culture is prevalent.
- *Creencia Fuerte en Dios*. Church support and belief in God. One strong asset of many Latino/a families is that parents have established support from a church and have strong religious beliefs (Gerner de Garcia, 2004).
- *Cuentos* (stories). Stories can show significant values in the culture and include heroes for students to emulate.
- *Dichos* (sayings). An example of a saying that encourages a commitment to the culture and moral values is *Quieres tapar el sol con un dedo* (You are trying to hide the sun with a finger). This means that you can't hide the truth for long.

Importantly, learning about Latino culture should not just occur at Cinco de Mayo, Latin National Hispanic Heritage month, or special holidays, but should be threaded throughout the curriculum as an important component of American culture.

While recognizing individual learning needs, there may also be ways of learning that are helpful to many Latino/a students. Gender may make a difference in how the teacher relates best to students. Romo (1998) suggested that Latinas can achieve higher graduation rates with mother-daughter programs that help girls and their mothers maintain interest in school.

> Teachers can connect with Latina students by making physical or eye contact, allowing Latinas ample time to answer questions, creating a sense of community and participation in the classroom, using examples in the classroom that are inclusive of Latinas, listening carefully and respectfully to students' questions and comments, and coaching students who seem reticent to speak (Romo, 1998, p. 2).

Many learners, male and female, appreciate the opportunity to be asked about their learning preference.

The students in our study all stated a preference for cooperative learning, group activities, and more involved types of learning. They resented being told to work independently and to simply read the text. Cooperative learning strategies, when used as intended with individual accountability included, have been proven to raise motivation and achievement in Latino/a students, especially English language learners. Since the implementation of NCLB in 2001 (NCLB, 2002), educators in our study reported that classroom practices have moved away from cooperative learning methods. Teachers felt pressure to teach only the material that the students will be tested on, and only in strictly prescribed ways. This shift made it difficult for classroom teachers to meet the need for group learning expressed by Latino/a youth.

Attention needs to also be given to the types of assessment that are used in the classroom. High expectations for academic success are critical, but there is a problem with advocating student learning that can *only* be tested through multiple-choice measures. Educators will likely see an improvement in learning when they find ways to use cooperative learning practices without sacrificing the need to prepare students for tests. A rich, culturally responsive curriculum and pedagogy can do more to raise test scores than "drill and kill" types of instruction.

Effective teachers engage in modeling and explanation to teach students. They stress higher-level thinking skills and active learning in heterogeneous settings where low-performing students are not excluded from these activities but encouraged to participate, and are supported in that act. These are all ways that help Latino/a learners flourish. Assigning independent work only after students are familiar with the concepts is cited as an effective strategy, as is role-playing and the use of simulation games. Teachers should assign projects that students can apply to their own cultural group, and provide an array of options for completing assignments. Accomplished teachers were found to provide more small-group than whole-group instruction, had students actively involved, and had a preferred teaching style of coaching as opposed to telling (Knapp, Shields, & Turnbull, 1995).

School administrators must be willing to modify the school curriculum to meet the needs of the Latino/a students in a particular school. Teachers would provide a wide set of culturally responsive instructional practices, including (1) instructional strategies that are congruent with the students' learning style, (2) cooperative learning, (3) the use of more than one language, and (4) the application of critical thinking skills. Teachers and their principals would advocate for the development of a pedagogy that welcomes students' languages, culture, and experiences into the school.

Offer caring that involves personalized care and high expectations

ACTION ITEM #5
Establishing a caring school classroom and overall school environment may be the most important work of a school administrator. Creating a safe school environment is a necessary and very elementary level of caring. Students who are harassed in hallways or feel unsafe in classrooms, as demonstrated in the case studies in this book, are in no position to engage in academic learning. Caring begins with student-centered administrators, teachers, and counselors who have an understanding of students' lives and an interest in learning more about them. Students cannot learn if they do not feel comfortable in the classroom and do not trust the teacher.

In *Eleven*, Sandra Cisneros (1991) recounted the story of Rachel, a young Latina who experiences embarrassment at the hands of an uncaring teacher. It is Rachel's birthday, but at school this fact is not disclosed. The day is overshadowed by the insistence that a ragged, smelly sweater that has been hanging in the classroom coat closet for months belongs to Rachel, despite Rachel's assertion that the ugly sweater does not belong to her. The teacher, Mrs. Price, loses patience with Rachel's denials and Rachel goes silent. "Because she's older and the teacher, she's right and I'm not" (p. 7).

Later, Mrs. Price angrily makes Rachel put the sweater on because Rachel has shoved it to the far corner of her desk. Humiliated, and forced to wear the dirty, foul garment, the child cries silent hot tears that are ignored. Later in the day, another child admits that the sweater belongs to her, and it quickly changes hands. The teacher pretends not to notice, but the birthday is ruined for Rachel.

> I'm eleven today. I'm eleven, ten, nine, eight, seven, six, five, four, three, two, and one, but I wish I was one hundred and two. I wish I was anything but eleven, because I want today to be far away already, far away like a runaway balloon, like a tiny *o* in the sky, so tiny-tiny you have to close your eyes to see it. (Cisneros, 1991, p. 7)

Few educators will admit to being uncaring. Caring is the hallmark of the teaching profession. Nevertheless, there are ways to care by being culturally responsive that have clearly not been implemented in some schools. Students in our study felt that they were "lesser kids" and largely ignored or that teachers actively disliked them. Everyone, teachers, administrators, counselors, school secretaries, custodians, and cooks have a role in creating a welcoming school where no one feels "lesser."

What is the most important thing classroom teachers can do to help Latino/a youth connect with the school and stay in school? The overwhelming response, from our study and from the research of many others (Anderson, 2006; G. Bell, 2004; Bowers & Flinders, 1990; Freire, 2004; Greene, 1995; Henry, 1996; Lee & Burkham, 2000; Noddings, 1992; Romo & Falbo, 1996; Witherell & Noddings, 1991) centered around the idea of caring and relationship building between teachers and students and their families. Lee and Burkham (2000) argued that their finding that "students are less likely to drop out of high schools where the average relationship between teachers and students (as perceived by the students) are more positive" (p. 25) is the most important finding of all.

Through collegial discussions and professional development, teachers can enhance their cultural responsiveness in the classroom. Teachers who are caring about the individuals they teach will be willing to learn the cultural information they need to teach in a relevant way and communicate better with Latino/a youth. Conversations about differences between individuals, affirming diversity as a strength, and acknowledgment of commonalities among classmates are important.

Establishing an environment of care requires teachers to put themselves in students' shoes and see what the school climate and culture looks like from their vantage point. Maria was staying up until midnight trying to get her homework done and was continually teased by classmates. Cristina and Cesar felt their teachers did not care for them at all. Sophia (who had once wanted to be a teacher) was told, "Here's the book. Do whatever you want."

And when she informed the school that she was leaving, the response was, "OK, just bring your books back." Armando said, "Schools treat Hispanics differently" (meaning they were meant to struggle on their own). Victor had potential as a soccer player but did not feel comfortable even talking to the coach. Silvia was excluded from the basketball team and was called a "spic," and no one seemed to care. Beatriz said, "Our class was just a bunch of Mexicans, so she [the teacher] hated our class." Enrique felt the school was glad to see him gone: His school principal "really wasn't going to do anything [to assist him] . . . Our stuff is limited straight out."

The findings of our study indicated that Latino/a youth may internalize a negative stereotype that contributes to dropping out of high school. Lockwood and Secada (1999), reporting on the work of the Hispanic Dropout Project, also found that stereotypes educators have about Latino/a students and their families impede academic progress. Educators need to be involved in asking themselves important questions about the way Latino/a students are viewed and how they are teaching them. When a student comments, "I'm just another Mexican. Why would they [teachers and administrators] care about me?" it is a sign that significant changes need to be made to the status quo. The lives of at-risk students are waiting to be turned around. This student might really be saying, "Why *don't* they care about me?" Ways to show caring need to be implemented. School must be made into a positive experience in the fight to keep Latino/a kids in school.

Some specific actions that could be taken to build positive student-teacher relationships, *con cariño*, are the following:

- Give individual attention and look for avenues of success for each student. School success is then redefined so that students will not see school achievement as selling out one's Latino/a cultural pride and values, *La Raza*, to "the Man" or "the White man's world." Building a foundation where there is a majority of successful Latino/a students in a class or school can be a way to accomplish this goal (Rodriguez, 2003).

- Look for opportunities for student successes not tied to grades as ways to demonstrate a caring environment. Success can come from student organizations, music, drama, athletics, and other nonacademic activities.

- Provide personal recognition and bonding activities, such as praise, outings, recognition ceremonies, certificates, and positive home calls to parents for meeting goals or improving behavior. These simple measures are aimed at increasing self-esteem, affiliation, and a sense of belonging with the school.

- Incorporate effective discipline measures, such as talking quietly and privately to misbehaving students, rather than sending them to the office, which students perceive as an uncaring act.
- Provide communication with students and families. School attendance was an issue for students in our study. Teachers and administrators did not take the time to communicate attendance and low grades to parents until it was too late—and even then parents were not personally contacted. Schools should be required to provide intensive period-by-period attendance monitoring and follow-ups with parents. If attendance is an issue, problem-solve the issue, which may mean offering a more flexible attendance policy or being creative to make attendance achievable.

Students need the support of caring relationships that includes modeling by adults and extending into peer relationships. Gibson, Gandara, and Koyama (2004, p. 11) noted that "students who experience a sense of belonging and peer acceptance in school are more likely to enjoy school, to be engaged academically, to participate in school activities, and to persist toward graduation and college." Our study showed that Latino/a youth tend to give up on school when they perceive teachers do not care about them. Central to caring is culturally responsive schooling as described and further elaborated in the leadership plan in this chapter and as advocated by Gay, 2000; Hollins and Oliver, 1999; Ladson-Billings, 1995; Nieto, 2004; Valdes, 1996; Valenzuela, 1999.

No to racism; anti-racist professional development

ACTION ITEM #6
Since the 1960s Civil Rights Movement, educational leaders have emphasized the promise that an education is the key to climbing the ladder to success. Yet today many students of color and low socioeconomic status still enter U.S. schools and realize that they are discriminated against. As Yolanda disclosed in Chapter 2, "I didn't know I was poor until I went to school." Shirley Chisholm, the first Black U.S. Congresswoman wrote: "Racism is so universal in this country, so widespread and deep-seated, that it is invisible because it is so normal" (ADL Curriculum Connections, 2005). It is not invisible to everyone, however. Latino/a youth in this study named teachers who they felt were racist and they recounted school situations that were racist, such as racial slurs, harassment, low expectations for the Latino/a students, and so on.

Critical in the quest to reduce the Latino/a dropout rate and to enhance learning opportunities for all students is to establish nonracist and caring classrooms and school cultures. One Idaho teacher taking a Multicultural Leadership course from Mary commented on her Latino/a students in the following way: "They hang around together and won't mix. They beat up on the White kids. They are always in trouble." Mary responded, "That's very interesting. Why do they hang out together?" The teacher answered, "They don't want to mix." The next question from Mary was, "What could you have done or someone else could have done to help students feel appreciated and begin to want to mix?" There was a long pause and the teacher stated that she would need some more time to think about this. She later admitted that she and other teachers had been viewing the Latino/a students negatively and that she would look for ways to foster success.

Antiracist training can be helpful for teachers and administrators who may be unaware of the powerful effects of their unconscious or conscious biases that lead to lowered expectations for Latino/a students and those with a low socioeconomic status. Consistent professional development is valuable when it promotes understanding and acceptance of diverse learning needs, and offers new strategies to meet those needs. "The tendency when we don't understand something is to claim it inferior or threatening. When we learn to value otherness or when we understand from within the ways of others, we can be accepting and appreciative" (Shabatay, 1991, p. 141).

Professional development can help teachers become aware of their own biases and stereotypes through role-playing situations and simulations. Today's educators must be on the lookout for individual and institutionalized racism. Systemic racism is more than the sum of individual prejudices and racism. The toll it takes on the self-efficacy of school-aged Latino/a youth is palpable. Teachers must respect and value all the cultural differences that children bring to the classroom. Students can then be carefully taught to respect each other and the differences in their communities. Teachers can embed learning activities into the daily curriculum that deliberately confront prejudice and intervene on the behalf of marginalized students.

One way to start professional development on antiracism might be within the collegial setting of individual rural schools. We can establish a climate of trust by accepting all participants' perspectives as valuable. Conversations about the issues surrounding Latino/a dropouts are necessary in order to seek student success. "When we take risks to talk about race and racism, we move into a realm in which we are not necessarily experts. As a result, we have to ask questions and expose our own learning process" (Bolgatz, 2005, p. 117). In a group or individually, educators might ask themselves questions such as the following: What knowledge do you have of the different cultural backgrounds of the students in your school? How would you get this knowledge? How do you find out about the impact of culture and language on learning? How do you affirm the cultural values of students? What do we need to do? How do we get what we need? These questions are clearly just a starting point, for there is much to discuss and discover. Antiracist strategies may include the following:

- Professional development for administrators, teachers, and counselors can be offered to examine their own personal biases and prejudices that we *all* have, and move to a position of antiracism and appreciation for others. Educators can start by considering the term *bias*: "an inflexible position or negative judgment about the nature, character and abilities of an individual and is based on a generalized idea about the group to which the person belongs" (Thiederman, 2003, p. 8). Other terms to explore include *prejudice* (negative opinion not based on evidence), *stereotyping* (fixed ideas about groups of people with no allowance for individual differences), and *racism* (view that one's own group or "race" is superior) (adapted from Anderson, 2006; Tiedt & Tiedt, 2005, p. 37). Nieto (2004) and Henze et al. (2002) also included terms and definitions that can be discussed. Thiederman (2003) offered cultural sensitivity exercises that could be used with staff and students. Appendix F provides both an excellent activity from the EdChange Multicultural Pavillion for colleagues to get to know one another, and an exercise developed by Anderson (2006) for staff to reflect on the diversity present in their personal lives. (Also see Anderson's Center for Racial Sensitivity at http://www.Idaho-crs.com.)
- Colleagues can observe classrooms and, in the process, document the patterns of teacher interaction with students. Bowers and Flinders (1990) noted that "as so many of the cultural patterns are invisible to the person who lives them as part of their everyday life, the third-party documentation will allow the teacher to escape a form of cultural blindness" (p. 190). We suggest the observer be from a different cultural background than the teacher observed.
- Multicultural literature can be included at all levels of the curriculum (preschool through high school), to help debunk stereotypes and undo prejudice and racism.
- Teachers can use film and videotape dramatizations of the harm caused by prejudice and the benefits of diversity. Such presentations have been found to engage viewers' feelings and enable them to see issues from different points of view. By engaging feelings as opposed to logical arguments or reasoning against injustices, people may change their actions. Teaching methods

can help students see the illogic and shallowness of prejudice. Counter-stereotyping activities can be helpful, such as focusing on Latina scientists, Jewish athletes, Black playwrights, and so on. These activities help students appreciate the diversity within racial and ethnic groups and reinforce the fact that they are not all alike.

A cautionary note is in order. Cross (2003) studied a multicultural education course in which teachers were exposed to others who were different from them. Although this lowered their fears and helped them develop some comfort in intercultural situations,

> a shift had not occurred from observation to engagement or dynamic cross-cultural interactions . . . they were still observing them [racial minority students] but not connecting with them; looking over or down on them, but not teaching them in culturally responsive ways. . . . The field experience did not influence their perceptions of what they should do in terms of curriculum, expectations and pedagogy, nor did what they had learned from them translate into considerations for the children they taught. (p. 207)

Learning to appreciate others involves more than a benefit to the educators themselves; it should translate into action and consideration for the students they teach. As an example of a lack of consideration, teachers may try to include diversity in the curriculum and not fully appreciate how that message is being portrayed to students of color. At Mary's son's school, the sixth graders were studying about the history of segregation and students had made posters reading "Whites only," which were publicized in hallways. For her son, who is African American, it was a visual reminder that he was in a group that was considered "lesser" at one time and it gave him heartache. The White students experienced no such heartache and this activity was planned more for their benefit. Students need to know history, but they also need to be told that segregation was immoral, that humans have made many mistakes and unjust laws throughout history, and that caring and social justice is a value we all need to hold.

Staff diversified; educators recruited, hired, retained, and promoted

ACTION ITEM #7

Latino/a role models, including bilingual teaching staff, mentors, and volunteers, were sorely needed in the rural schools we studied. Sophia said, "You don't see any Mexicans teaching because—I don't know why. I don't remember not even one teacher being Hispanic in any school I've been in. Not principals either." In this study of three high schools and three alternative schools there were no Latina/o administrators and only two teachers. Adolescents are keenly aware of how others perceive them, and Latino/a students see that they are not well represented in the field of education. The absence of successful Latino/a role models presents another identity barrier for students to overcome. According to Nakkula (2003), identity is developed through an ongoing process that integrates "successes, failures, routines, habits, rituals, novelties, thrills, threats, violations, gratifications, and frustrations into a coherent and evolving interpretation of who we are" (p. 7).

Awareness of race or social class affects identity formation and feelings of self-efficacy. In an interview with social workers in a socioeconomically diverse high school, Sadowski (2003) found that Latino/a students already had a sense that the only adult in the school that they could identify with was the custodian. "These kids are not stupid; they know that most of the Spanish-speaking people here live in certain parts of town and hold certain types of jobs. It's very difficult for them to overcome that" (p. 125).

Recruiting Latino/a educators has been difficult not just for rural schools, but for schools across the nation. "Hispanics represent only 2.9% of public school teachers and 2.8% of private school teachers" (Hodgkinson & Outtz, 1996, p. 20). However, culturally responsive leaders can use creativity to increase diversity in staffing. Latino/a community members, parents, and graduates of HEP (High School Equivalency) programs could be invited into the school and offered stipends to work as tutors or mentors. And the "grow your own" pipeline from Latino parent to paraprofessional to teacher to administrator is a strategy that many school districts could use. Mary saw this policy implemented successfully in Washington state, where many Latino/a paraprofessionals worked their way up through the system to become teachers, principals, and central office administrators.

One does not have to be Latino to influence the success of Latino students, which is just as well because 85–90% of teachers nationwide are White (NEA, 2006a, p. 5). Gay (2000), referring to what she called "professional racism," asserted that educators who believe that only Latino educators can successfully deal with Latino students make a

> very fallacious and dangerous assumption. It presumes that membership in an ethnic group is necessary or sufficient to enable teachers to do effective, culturally proficient pedagogy. . . . All teachers, regardless of their ethnic-group membership, must be taught how to do, and be held accountable for doing, culturally responsive teaching for diverse students, just as all students from all

ethnic and racial groups must be held accountable for high-level achievement and provided means to accomplish it. (Gay, 2000, pp. 205–206)

It is important to actively diversify the teaching staff and ensure that all teachers are highly qualified and have the cultural and linguistic knowledge and skills that they need to reach Latino/a youth. Where Latino/a staff do exist, others in the schools need to pay attention to not just hiring Latino/as into the teaching force but also mentoring them. (See Gardiner et al., 2000, for more on mentoring school leaders of color.)

Finally, it needs to be remembered that a diverse teaching and administrative force benefits all students, not just Latinos. A diverse staff provides essential exposure to different ideas, experiences, and worldviews (Adam, 2006). How can we be considered educated if we do not know how to communicate with and appreciate the wide variety of people who make up our pluralistic U.S. society and the world?

Implement heterogeneous classes with differentiated instruction

ACTION ITEM #8

We found in this study that Latino/a students do not want to be set apart from the larger U.S. group, either as being different or as standing out in some way. They want to be like everyone else and not be in a lower-tracked class for "dumb kids and Mexicans" (Beatriz). Manning and Baruth (2000) found that Latino/a students do not want to be set apart from the group, either as being different or as excelling. Students in our study felt devalued by the current practice of tracking. In tracking, students are divided into two groups: those designated for the academic track and are bound for college, and those who are tracked for vocational jobs through less abstract courses such as auto shop, carpentry, and typing. The problem is that there is little fluidity or change in group membership, making it very difficult for students who are quite possibly misidentified to move out of the track. Sophia noted, "Our class was a bunch of Mexicans, so she [the teacher] hated our class."

Social relationships were very important to the students in our study and heterogeneously grouped classes with differentiated instruction and cooperative learning activities can be a way to meet the learning needs of all students, by allowing teachers to focus on individual learning needs and to provide for continuous progress and advancement. Burris, Heubert, and Levin (2006) found that heterogeneous grouping increased completion of advanced math courses for *all* students, including those who were not students of color and or from low socioeconomic backgrounds. Classes that are heterogeneously and ethnically mixed allow students opportunities to build long-term, sustained, inter-ethnic, and interracial friendships.

As a beginning step, administrators can examine the data and see if there are inequities ethnically or socioeconomically in how students are grouped together, and then set about correcting these injustices. If Latina/o students are not equally represented (or worse, not represented at all) in advanced placement classes or merit scholar and honors programs, then this situation can be changed using a leadership plan for culturally responsive schools. Differentiated instruction can be a way to allow teachers to attend to the individualized learning needs of students within the regular heterogeneously grouped classroom. (For information on differentiated instruction, see Hall, 2002; Tomlinson, 2003; Tomlinson & McTighe, 2006). High expectations for learning are a critical element of differentiated instruction. Caring is not coddling or excusing poor work. Victor, for instance, felt the work at his high school was "too easy." Caring means holding high expectations and simultaneously providing the tools for success by motivating and guiding students. Students can be motivated one step at a time, by using culturally relevant material and approaches, and building on prior background knowledge and successes.

An excellent example of how a teacher can hold high expectations for all students and simultaneously differentiate instruction according to their needs is provided in the work of Idaho science teacher, Mr. John M. (Mick) Sharkey, teaching in a small rural school, Parma High School. The school in which he teaches is diverse: 67% White, 31% Latino, and 63% of the students eligible for free or reduced lunch. Mick was awarded the Idaho Teacher of the Year Award in 2006, an award presented by the Idaho Education Association. At the award ceremony, students and parents of all ethnicities and socioeconomic backgrounds celebrated Mick for his outstanding achievements in science. The audience resembled a rainbow coalition, no small feat for Idaho, which is a predominantly White state. What drew all these supporters of Mr. Sharkey to the celebration was the knowledge that he believed in his heart that all his students were capable of learning at a high level of academic achievement. He accomplished this outcome through getting to know the students well, differentiating instruction according to their prior background knowledge and interests, and motivating students through application of knowledge into real-world situations. Parents and students alike loved this teacher for his faith in them, his ability to draw out their interests, and his appreciation of students for who they are, not for what they can accomplish. In turn, students responded by dreaming big and delivering on that promise. (For an interview with Mr. Sharkey, see Anderson, 2006).

Vary counseling roles beyond career counseling

ACTION ITEM #9

Students in our study went through their entire schooling careers with very few mentors. Educators did not connect with them and counselors were not available to assist them through the most difficult situations. Even the most advantaged youth would have had difficulty navigating the challenges of homelessness, failing grades, or teen pregnancy without the support of a caring adult. The Ennis High School principal said that the school counselors, "spend a lot of time with scheduling and when they do counseling it is mainly career counseling for kids that need help getting into college. We really don't see our high school counselors getting into the personal lives of most students. And if there are discipline issues, the vice principal takes care of it." Students in our study desperately needed the kind of help that schools could have provided by dedicating the time of one counselor on staff. Assistance to get into college is helpful, but students needed help first to be on track to graduate from high school. In addition, they needed information on courses to take and career options. Career Pathways is an established federal reform, with high tech courses leading to careers as medical technicians, computer networkers, and surgical technicians. The problem is that in the rural schools we studied, few Latino/a students were offered this information or these opportunities.

Latino/a students, like all students, need positive role models in their life, adults who care for them and connect with them. Counselors have a key role to play in assisting students to complete school (Stanard, 2003). Counselors have the opportunity to be a caring adult in the lives of students and to encourage school success. They can encourage friendship groups across ethnic lines and work to alleviate many of the relational and personal kinds of issues that affect school performance. Research shows that caring adult relationships are critical for school success. For example, Wehlage (1989), in a study of 14 junior high and high schools that were using innovative methods to address problems, found that careful attention by adults to social relationships produced continued school membership for at-risk students. Having a significant adult role model made a difference for most youth. Counselors, teachers, and administrators could all fill this role.

Skills development training conducted by the school counselor could also be helpful in the area of motivation. Coupled with new school policies that foster Latino/a involvement in extracurricular activities, training could help students focus on the goal of school graduation and see it as achievable. Nesman et al., (2001) studied successful Latino/a students and found that the major contributors to their success in school included "a personal motivation to succeed, supportive parents, and being interested in and involved in school activities" (p. 5).

Latino/a youth are subject to all the cultural and social influences that surround people their age. Attitudes, habits, and relationships with others are adopted and rejected continuously. Teachers of these youth can attest to the fact that young people change friends, personalities, and their minds like they change their clothes. It is a time of turmoil, even in the best of circumstances. For Latino/a adolescents, the decision to drop out of high school can be more about battle fatigue than academic failure. The battlefield is the social arena of school and community. Home is the place to rest up for the next campaign, but home becomes less of a respite for those who find home life unstable or unfriendly. Establishing school connections with mental health and community counselors may help address issues outside the school that affect school performance and retention.

Counselors and teachers have a responsibility to be aware of students and their challenges. It is telling that not one of the students in this study spoke to a teacher or counselor about his or her problems and challenges even though they were considerable (e.g., exclusion from sports and other activities that they loved due to failing grades or inability to pay fees, homelessness, failing grades, fights with peers, drug addiction, teachers who were verbally insulting, teen pregnancy). Some problems were school-based and some were home-based. These youth did not seem to know how the educational system works and were struggling without the help of caring adults in the system. Not one of these students spoke with school personnel about his or her decision to drop out prior to the act. And some school personnel facilitated the students' exit from schools, without a word of encouragement to stay. School counselors, with the support of their administrators, could have provided valuable counseling to these teens in social skills development, job skills training, school rules, study skills, and ways to enhance success. They could also have personally contacted parents.

Every parent valued

ACTION ITEM #10
Latino families value education highly (Cooper et al., 1999; Ramirez, 2003; Sosa, 1996), but they simply may not always have had good relationships with schools. Students in this study spoke about schools as disconnected from their families. Parents were never contacted personally about attendance, slipping grades, or other issues. One way administrators can try to establish connections with the Latino/a community is by offering personal

invitations for parents or community members to visit or volunteer for some activity at school (Weiner, Leighton, & Funkhouse, 2000; Osterling & Garza, 2004). Care needs to be taken to find activities that are valued by the Latino community, for example, a soccer event.

Opportunities for meaningful involvement by parents should be more than providing cookies or listening to children read. Parents cannot be given a seat at the decision-making table if there is no table. Educators need to push aside their fears, if they have them, get to know their brothers and sisters who are Latino/a, and make room for them. Classes can also be offered by the district for parents, such as English classes or how to help students with homework (Abrego, Rubin, & Sutterby, 2005; Cooper et al., 1999; C. Ferguson, 2004, 2005). However, the instructor would need to be accepted by the community and not present the "American" way as better (Trumbull et al., 2001).

Parents of Latino/a youth may also need different forms of home-school engagement than are currently practiced in rural schools and communities. Lopez (2003a) used the example of parents taking children to work to learn vocational skills and also to teach them the value of an education through the example of their own struggles. In our study, many of the students had experiences working alongside their parents laboring in the fields, onion and cherry sheds, and dairies. Yet the schools did not value these experiences at all. Sophia put it this way, "I didn't want to quit, but I didn't have anything to do with it. There was nothing for me out of it. I went to work [in the potato harvest] for her [mother] for a month" (Sophia). Missing a month of school caused Sophia to lose credit for that semester of her junior year. This is an example of disconnection between the practical needs of families and the policies of schools.

Respect for students and their families is essential and administrators need to have the understanding that students and their parents may have been disrespected in the past (Salend & Taylor, 1993). Espinosa's study (1995) showed that parents can be easily intimidated by school authorities, a fact that savvy administrators need to be aware of and consciously work to overcome (also see Onikama, Hammond, & Koki [n.d.]; Sosa, 1996). Fowler-Finn (2003) noted the value of listening to students and their families and the effect this can have on closing the achievement gap. School personnel actively listening to students and their families and finding out their perspectives, needs, desires, and challenges is key to a respectful relationship. Administrators could provide the resources, personnel, and transportation for building these improved student-family-school connections.

The concept of machismo means a strong commitment to respect the tradition of chivalry, not male dominance. The mother, as the matriarch of the family, is in a highly respected position. Latino/as have a strong commitment to their home language, and extended family and kinship networks are highly valued. Latino/a parents respond warmly to kindness. Signs of respect, like making the parents and any other family members accompanying them feel very welcome when they come to school, go a long way toward gaining support. Of course, these are generalities and are not intended to be true for every Latino/a in every school.

Respect for the parents has to be demonstrated. It is sometimes customary for rural schools, if they employ a Spanish-speaking or Latina/o educator at all, to delegate the responsibility for the school's Latina/o youth to that person. Doing so robs other administrators and teachers of the opportunity to show respect. This is a loss for both educators and parents. Gay (2000) admonished White teachers not to rely on Latina/o teachers to take care of all the Latina/o students in school. This sends a message that White educators are not sufficiently well prepared and do not care to work with Latina/o students and families. Culturally responsive, high-quality instruction designed to meet the needs of the diversity within our schools is everyone's responsibility.

Latino/a parents may feel initial distrust for White professionals. This may be misinterpreted by educators that they are not as interested in the academic achievement of their children as their White counterparts. We must be careful not to misinterpret the difference between the school involvement of White parents and Latino/a parents as lack of concern, because this is not the case. Latino/a parents think of teachers as experts in their children's education. They have respect (*respeto*) for authority, and may feel they are showing disrespect to the teacher by asking too many questions about the educational experience of their child. Teachers are often unaware of the honorable position they hold in the eyes of Latino/a parents.

Imagine how you would feel if someone you regarded highly not only ignored you, but also treated your children badly, and made them feel stupid or bad. If you can imagine this, then you can probably understand why some Latino/a parents are reluctant to make contact with the teacher with whom their child is having problems. "It can also be painful to realize how racist the world is. Guilt and anger are important markers. They alert us to the need to find new ways to respond to our own racism and internalized oppression so that we can help our students do the same" (Bolgatz, 2005, p. 115). Fear of those who are different and unknown is also at play here.

Building positive rewards and communication with parents regarding homework projects, activities, and accomplishments is helpful. Be aware of the demands on the parents' time and make the assignments achievable by students with limited monitoring, or provide school homework tutorials after school where students can complete their work. For instance, Maria was staying up until midnight trying to complete homework for which she was unprepared. Cesar said he would have attended after-school tutoring if it had been provided. Cesar's parents had to choose between employment and participation in their children's school experiences. For an unskilled worker the threat of replacement for absences is real and other employment hard to find.

Reach out and attend out-of-school events, like *Quincineras* (Sweet 15) and cultural fairs. We have been invited to participate in these events, and have found them valuable in opening doors to conversations about the lives of students and their beliefs and aspirations. These are opportunities that educators must seek out and explore, for they demonstrate caring. "Parents are to be respected for the knowledge that they have as parents, irrespective of how that differs from the school view of 'good parenting'" (Henry, 1996, p. 189).

Child advocacy by administrators and teachers is an essential role if Latino/a parents are to trust administrators. Parents may not feel comfortable advocating for their children as it may be considered disrespectful (Milian, 1999; Osterling & Garza, 2004). As mentioned earlier, *respeto* is a key cultural term. Administrators must take an advocacy role for Latino/a students and build trust with Latino/a parents, rather than impose a traditional model of parent involvement.

Parents have an enormous influence on the outcomes of their children, but too often the power of classroom teachers to make the lives of children heaven or hell is overlooked, except by people who have had experiences like Rachel's (Cisneros, 1991). We do not believe that the vast majority of educators intentionally treat Latino/a students poorly. However, teachers who are found to be racist, impatient, inflexible, or quick to show disapproval toward Latino families or students should be retrained, reassigned, or removed.

SUMMARY

Students' own words in this study showed that the students were seeking higher levels of caring, empathy, mentoring, guidance, and connection between their families and the schools. Principals and teachers in this study primarily saw the students who dropped out as troublemakers; the students saw the educators as unresponsive and uncaring. The value of this study is that it shows educators what students feel; it makes the students' experiences real. If we had studied successful Latina/o students we would have had very different results, which might have given the impression that schools attend well to their Latina/o students and families. The high dropout numbers tell a different story. We have shown the wisdom of the students and their powerful critique of the school system's incompatibility to meet their needs. The students were ready for a deeper level of discussion that never happened. If educators and school leaders are open to the voices of their students and their critique a wonderful opportunity presents itself for relevant education.

We have also presented a culturally responsive leadership plan that principals and superintendents can use to reduce Latino/a school dropout and simultaneously establish a positive school environment for *all* students. The plan would be customized to a particular setting, include measurable benchmarks for success, and monitored at the beginning, middle, and end of an evaluation period.

Educators, through professional development, can be taught how to be aware of areas of conflict between Latino cultural values and the way schools are operating, and then set out to become culturally responsive. Schools can be reorganized to be culturally responsive in ways that keep kids from dropping out. Diversity, acceptance, and communication are ways to cultivate success for *all*. Latino/a students should not have to feel that they are being forced to give up their cultural and social roots to achieve school success.

Other students benefit by gaining an education that is more complete and grounded in the contributions of *all* Americans. Educators who get to know their students and build significant caring relationships with them will be able to help Latino/a students stay in school and gain the skills they need to be successful. The focus on building a culturally responsive school is consistent with research that shows that when schools focus on a rich, engaging, multicultural curriculum, test scores rise. For example, as shown in Smith's (2002) study of a bilingual education program in Tucson, Arizona, test scores rose when the focus was not on the tests, but instead on a lively and engaging educational environment that enhanced students' confidence and abilities as bilingual and bi-literate students in the world.

Motivating students and inspiring *ganas* (will or desire) to achieve academically will only occur when we have educators *con cariño* (with loving respect) who are willing to provide a culturally responsive education. The NCLB Act provides sanctions to schools who fail to deliver educational success to all groups of students, and in that sense it has certainly gained our attention. However, it is punitive and does not provide the necessary resources for success. We need to try some new approaches. Educators want success for Latino/a students, but traditional methods have yielded traditional results of a continuing problem with high school dropout rates.

For administrators, teachers, or counselors seeking to enhance the success of Latina/o youth, this book provides resources in culturally responsive leadership to assist in that goal. While the dominant literature emphasizes that there is something wrong with students and their families, we think instead that taking the students' perspectives, as we have done in this book, offers a tremendous opportunity to address the dropout problem in the United States. The students in our study guided us in developing the leadership plan for culturally responsive schools. Whether the plan will work rests on the willingness of educators on the frontline to try it out and adapt it to their own situations. The 85–90% of teachers in the United States who are White, teaching the 40–60% of students of color (NEA, 2006a, p. 5), have a choice to make. They can be color-blind and shatter dreams, or they can be culturally responsive to their students and "dreamkeepers" (Ladson-Billings, 1994).

A leadership plan such as this one is very different from the strategic plans found in most schools. The focus in this book is on developing teachers and staff to be multiculturally responsive and antiracist. Culturally responsive leadership is about educators seeking understanding of the ways of knowing and background knowledge of their diverse students; it can have a powerful impact on whether or not children feel welcome and valued in the hours they attend school. It can have an impact on the families the children return to at the end of the day, and whether or not they feel welcomed in the community. There is a ripple effect here that must not be ignored. Teachers, counselors, and school administrators can make the difference in whether a student succeeds or fails. Silvia's poem that follows describes the pain of one high school student who had her dream shattered.

High School
You are judged by things such as clothes or race.
You have the high class and the low class.
And a lot of teachers and administrators
Will work with the kids
That help the school reputation, like in athletics or academic-wise.
But the lesser kids,
The kids who aren't really involved with the school
But want to do well in school,
Aren't really encouraged.
I was definitely low on the food chain.

References

Abrego, M., Rubin, R., & Sutterby, J. (2005). Opening doors to Latino Families. *English Language Learners*, 8(5). Retrieved March 13, 2006, from http://www.alasweb.org/TemplateMari/Socio-Economic-Religious/Opening%20Doors%20to%20Latino%20Families.doc

Adam, M. (2006, March). AAC&U Reports on the Diversity/Excellence Connection. *Hispanic Outlook*, 16(12), 15–17.

ADL Curriculum Connections, (2005). Shirley Chisolm: Unbought, Unbossed, and Unforgotten. Retrieved July 2, 2007, from www.adl.org/education/curriculum_connections/lesson_chisolm.asp

Almeida, C., Johnson, C., & Steinberg, A. (2006). Making good on a promise: What policymakers can do to support the educational persistence of dropouts. *Creating strategies for educational and economic opportunity*. Retrieved November 21, 2006, from the Jobs for the Future Web site: http://www.jff.org/JFF_KC_Pages.php?WhichLevel=1&lv1_id=4&lv2_id=0&lv3_id=0&KC_M_ID=287

Ambrosio, J. (2004). No child left behind: The case of Roosevelt High School. *Phi Delta Kappan*, 85(9), 709–712.

Anaya, R. (1995). *Bless me Ultima*. New York: Wagner Books.

Anderson, K. (2006). *Teacher communication with students from diverse backgrounds*. Unpublished doctoral dissertation, Moscow: University of Idaho.

Aronson, J., & Good, C. (2002). The development and consequences of stereotype vulnerability in adolescents. In F. Pajares & T. Urdan (Eds.), *Academic motivation of adolescents* (pp. 299–330). Greenwich, CN: Information Age.

Astone, N., & McLanahan, S. (1994). Family structure, residential mobility, and school dropout: A research note. *Demography*, 31(4), 575–584.

Banks, J. (2006). *Cultural diversity and education: Foundations, curriculum and teaching.* Boston: Pearson Education.

Banks, J., & Banks, C. (Eds.). (2001). *Handbook of research on multicultural education.* San Francisco: Jossey-Bass.

Bell, G. (2004). What caring looks like in the classroom: How a teacher goes about his day to meet the needs of his students. Moscow: University of Idaho.

Bell, L. (2002). Sincere fictions: The pedagogical challenges of preparing white teachers for multicultural classrooms. *Equity & Excellence in Education, 35*(3), 236–244.

Bhanpuri, H., & Reynolds, G. (2003). *Understanding and addressing the issue of high school dropout age.* Naperville, IL: Learning Point Associates.

Bolgatz, J. (2005). *Talking race in the classroom.* New York: Teachers College Press.

Bowers, C. A., & Flinders, D. J. (1990). *Responsive teaching: An ecological approach to classroom patterns of language, culture, and thought.* New York: Teachers College Press.

Burris, C., Heubert, J., & Levin, H. (2006). Accelerating mathematic achievement using heterogeneous grouping. *American Educational Research Journal, 43*(1), 105–136.

California Tomorrow. (2002, April). The high-quality learning conditions needed to support students of color and immigrants at California community colleges. Paper presented at the California Joint Legislation Committee. Sacramento, CA: Carol Dowell.

Capper, C. (1993). *Educational administration in a pluralistic society.* Albany: State University of New York Press.

Carlson, L. (Ed.). (1994). *Cool salsa: Bilingual poems on growing up Latino in the United States.* New York: Henry Holt.

Carlson, L. (Ed.). (2005). *Red hot salsa: Bilingual poems on being young and Latino in the United States.* New York: Henry Holt.

Carrasquillo, A. (1994). A rationale for Hispanic representation in instructional materials. *The Journal of Educational Issues of Language Minority Students, 14,* 115–126.

Carter, P. (2005). *Keepin' it real: School success beyond black and white.* New York: Oxford University Press.

Ceja, M. (2004). Chicana college aspirations and the role of parents: Developing educational resiliency. *Journal of Hispanic Education, 3*(4), 339–358.

Center for Applied Linguistics. (2005). *Directory of two-way bilingual immersion programs in the U.S.* Retrieved March 4, 2005, from http://www.cal.org.twi/directory/

Child Trends Data Bank. (2006). *High school dropout rates*. Retrieved June 19, 2006, from http://www.childtrendsdatabank.org/indicators/1HighSchoolDropout.cfm

Cisneros, S. (1984). *The house on Mango Street*. New York: Vintage Books.

Cisneros, S. (1991). *Woman hollering creek and other stories*. New York: Vintage Contemporaries.

Clarke, M., Abrams, L., & Madaus, G. (2001). The effects and implications of high stakes achievement tests for adolescents. In T. Urdan & F. Pajares (Eds.), *Adolescence and education: Vol. 1*. Greenwich, CN: Information Age.

Colangelo, N., & Davis, G. (2003). *Handbook of gifted education* (3rd ed.). Needham Heights, MA: Allyn & Bacon.

Conchas, G. (2006). *Color of success: Race and high-achieving urban youth*. New York: Teachers College Press.

Cooper, C., Denner, J., & Lopez, E. (1999). Cultural brokers: Helping Latino children on pathways toward success. *The Future of Children—When School Is Out, 9*(2), 51–57.

Creswell, J. (1998). *Qualitative inquiry and research design: Choosing among five traditions*. Thousand Oaks, CA: Sage.

Creswell, J. W. (2002). *Educational research: Planning, conducting, and evaluating quantitative and qualitative research*. Upper Saddle River, NJ: Merrill Prentice Hall.

Cross, B. (2003). Learning or unlearning racism: Transferring teacher education curriculum to classroom practices. *Theory Into Practice, 42*(2), 203–209.

Delgado-Gaitan, C. (1988). The value of conformity: Learning to stay in school. *Anthropology & Education Quarterly, 19*(4), 354–381.

Delgado-Gaitan, C. (2006). *Building culturally responsive classrooms: A guide for K-6 teachers*. Thousand Oaks, CA: Sage.

Delpit, L. (1995). *Other people's children: Cultural conflict in the classroom*. New York: The New Press.

Delpit, L., & Dowdy, J. (Eds.). (2003). *The skin that we speak: Thoughts on language and culture in the classroom*. New York: The New Press.

D'Emilio, B. (2002). Action research on meaningful family involvement by parents, teachers and students: Using the telling strategically. *Penn GSE Perspectives on Urban Education, 1*(2), 1–7. Retrieved November, 10, 2005, from www.urbanjournal.org

DiMaria, F. (2004). Unreliable, unassessed, and intolerable: The elusive high school dropout count. *The Hispanic Outlook in Higher Education, 14*(23), 20–22. Retrieved December 11, 2004, from http://ida.lib.uidaho.edu:2051

District Profile. 2005. www.sde.state.id.us

Dorfman, D., & Fisher, A. (2002). Building relationships for student success: School-family-community partnerships and student achievement in the Northwest. *Northwest Regional Educational Laboratory.* (ERIC Document Reproduction service No. ED474379) Retrieved December, 12, 2005, from http://www.nwrel.org/partnerships/cloak/booklet2.pdf

Dornbusch, S. M., & Kaufman, J. G. (2001). The social structure of the American high school. In T. Urdan & F. Pajares (Eds.), *Adolescence and Education: Vol. 1.* Greenwich, CN: Information Age.

Dutton, D., & Humphries, C. (1994). *A rendezvous with Idaho history.* Boise: Sterling Ties.

Echevarria, J., Vogt, M., & Short, D. (2004). *Making content comprehensible for English learners: The SIOP model* (2nd ed.). Boston: Pearson Education.

Edley, C., Jr., & Wald, J. (2003). *The hidden dropout crisis.* Retrieved December 28, 2004, from www.americanprogress.org The Civil Rights Project at Harvard University Web site.

EdChange Multicultural Pavillion. (2005). Awareness activities. Retrieved June 22, 2006, from http://www.edchange.org/multicultural/activityarch.html

The Education Alliance. (2006). *The knowledge loom: Educators sharing and learning together.* Retrieved June, 16, 2006, from http://knowledge loom.org/

Education Trust. (2003). Telling the whole truth (or not) about high school graduation rates. Retrieved September 12, 2004, from www.sde.state.id.us/finance/dropout.asp

Erickson, F. (1993). Transformation and school success: The politics and culture of educational achievement. In e. Jacob & C. Jordan (Eds.), *Minority education: Anthropological perspective* (pp. 27–52). Norwood, NJ: Ablex.

Erikson, E. H. (1968). *Identity, youth, and crisis.* New York: W. W. Norton.

Espinosa, L. (1995). *Hispanic parent involvement in early childhood programs* (Report No. EDO-PS-95-3). Urbana, IL: Clearinghouse on Elementary and Early Childhood Education. (ERIC Document Reproduction Service No. ED382412)

Ferguson, A. (2001). *Bad boys: Public schools in the making of black masculinity.* Ann Arbor: University of Michigan.

Ferguson, C. (2004). Learning outside the classroom: What teachers can do to involve family in supporting classroom instruction. *Southwest Educational Development Laboratory (SEDL).* Retrieved October 15, 2005, from the National Center for Family and Community Connections

With Schools Web site: http://www.sedl.org/connections/resources/rb/research-brief2.pdf

Ferguson, C. (2005). Reaching out to diverse populations: What can schools do to Foster family-school connections? *Southwest Educational Development Laboratory (SEDL)*. Retrieved October 15, 2005, from the National Center for Family and Community Connections With Schools Web site: http://www.sedl.org/connections/resources/rb/rb5–diverse.pdf

Fine, M. (1991). *Framing dropouts: Notes on the politics of an urban public high school*. Albany: State University of New York Press.

Fine, M., & Burns, A. (2003). Class notes: Toward a critical psychology of class and schooling. *Journal of Social Issues*, 59(4), 841. Retrieved January 11, 2005, from www.questia.com

Fowler-Finn, T. (2003). Listening to minority students: One district's approach to closing the achievement gap. In M. Sadowski (Ed.), *Adolescents at school: Perspectives on youth, identity, and education*. Cambridge, MA: Harvard Education Press.

Frankenberg, R. (1993). *White women, race matters: The social construction of whiteness*. Minneapolis: University of Minnesota Press.

Freire, P. (2001). *Pedagogy of the oppressed*. New York: Continuum.

Freire, P. (2004). *Pedagogy of hope*. New York: Continuum.

Fry, R. (2002). *The changing landscape of American public education: New students, new schools*. Washington, DC: Pew Hispanic Center.

Fry, R. (2003). *Hispanic youth dropping out of U.S. schools: Measuring the challenge*. Washington, D.C.: Pew Hispanic Center.

Gamache, S. (2006, June 6). Brit dubs Risch chief of Bushlandia. *Idaho Statesman*, A, p. 1.

Garcia, C. (2006, November 4). An analysis of critical race theory and its applicability to under-achievement and social resistance of Latina/o students. Paper presented at the annual meeting of the American Educational Studies Association (AESA), Spokane, WA.

Garcia Lorca, F. (2001). *Blood wedding*. (L. Groag, Trans.). New York: Dramatists Play Service.

Gardiner, M., & Enomoto, E. (2006). Urban school principals and their role as multicultural leaders. *Urban Education*, 41(6), 560–584.

Gardiner, M., Enomoto, E., & Grogan, M. (2000). *Coloring outside the lines: Mentoring women into school leadership*. Albany: State University of New York Press.

Gay, G. (2000). *Culturally responsive teaching: Theory, research & practice*. New York: Teachers College Press.

Gerner de Garcia, B. (2004). *Literacy for Latino deaf and hard-of-hearing English language learners: Building the knowledge base*. Presentation at the

Gallaudet Research Institute. Retrieved December, 15, 2005, from http://gri.gallaudet.edu/Presentations/2004–04–07–2.pdf

Gibson, M., Gandara, P., & Koyama, J. (2004). The role of peers in the schooling of U.S. Mexican youth. In M. Gibson, P. Gandara, & P. Koyama (Eds.), *U.S. Mexican youth, peers and school achievement* (pp. 1–17). New York: Teachers College Press.

Giorgi, A. (Ed.). (1985). *Phenomenology and psychological research.* Pittsburg, PA: Duquesne University Press.

Gollnick, D., & Chinn, P. (2006). *Multicultural education in a pluralistic society* (7th ed.). Columbus, OH: Pearson.

Gonzales, M. (2002). Successfully educating Latinos: The pivotal role of the principal. In M. Gonzales, A. Huerta-Macias, & J. Villamil Tinajero (Eds.), *Educating Latino students: A guide to successful practice* (pp. 3–28). Lanham, MD: Scarecrow Press.

Gonzales, M., Huerta-Macias, A., & Villamil Tinajero, J. (Eds.). (2002). *Educating Latino students: A guide to successful practice.* Lanham, MD: Scarecrow Press.

Greene, M. (1995). *Releasing the imagination: Essays on education, the arts, and social change.* San Francisco: Jossey-Bass.

Griggs, S., & Dunn, R. (1996). *Hispanic-American students and learning style.* ERIC Digest. (ERIC Document Reproduction Service No. ED393607)

Groenewald, T. (2004). A phenomenological research design illustrated. *International Journal of Qualitative Methods, 3*(4). Retrieved November 16, 2004, from www.alberta.ca/~iiqm/backissues/3_1/pdf/groenewald.pdf

Hall, T. (2002). *Differentiated instruction.* Wakefield, MA: National Center on Assessing the General Curriculum. Retrieved November 1, 2006, from http://www.cast.org/publications/ncac/ncac_diffinstruc.html

Halle, T., & LeMenestrel, S. (1999). *How do social, economic, and cultural factors influence fathers' involvement with their children?* Research Brief. Washington, DC: Child Trends. (ERIC Document Reproduction Service No. ED442550)

Hauser, R. (2000, October). *Race-ethnicity, social background, and grade retention.* Paper presented at the Laboratory for Student Success at Temple University, Philadelphia, PA.

Henry, M. (1993). *School cultures: Universes of meaning in private schools.* Norwood, NJ: Ablex.

Henry, M. (1996). *Parent-school collaboration: Feminist organizational structures and school leadership.* Albany: State University of New York Press.

Henze, R., Katz, A., & Norte, E. (2002). *Leading for diversity: How school leaders promote positive interethnic relations*. Thousand Oaks, CA: Corwin Press.

Hess, R. (2000). Dropping out among Mexican American youth: Review of the literature through an ecological perspective. *Journal of Education for Students Placed at Risk, 5*(3), 267–290.

Hondo, C. (2005). *A phenomenological investigation of Hispanic high school dropouts from rural communities in the context of No Child Left Behind*. Unpublished doctoral dissertation. Moscow: University of Idaho.

Hodgkinson, H., & Obarakpor, A. (1994). *The invisible poor: Rural youth in America*. Washington, DC: Institute for Educational Leadership. (ERIC Document Reproduction Service No. ED375995)

Hodgkinson, H., & Outtz, J. (1996). *Hispanic Americans: A look back, a look ahead*. Washington, DC: Institute for Educational Leadership. (ERIC Document Reproduction Service No. ED393959)

Hollins, E., & Oliver, E. (1999). *Pathways to success in school: Culturally responsive teaching*. Mahway, NJ: Erlbaum.

Hopkins, R. (1994). *Narrative schooling: Experiential learning and the transformation of American education*. New York: Teachers College Press.

Howard, G. (2006). *We can't teach what we don't know: White teachers, multiracial schools*. New York: Teachers College Press.

Hurston, Z. (2006). *Their eyes were watching God*. New York: HarperCollins.

Idaho Commission on Hispanic Affairs. (2004). *Hispanic profile data book for Idaho*. Retrieved May 2, 2006, from http://www2.state.id.us/icha

Idaho Commission on Hispanic Affairs. (2007). Hispanic profile data book for Idaho. Retrieved July 2, 2007, from http://www2.state.id.us/icha

Idaho Foundation Standards for school leaders. (2007). Retrieved July 3, 2007, from www.sde.idaho..gov/certification/default.asp

Idaho Kids Count. (2005). *Data book. Statistics on family and community in Idaho*. Retrieved June 18, 2006, from http://www.idahokidscount.org/

Idaho State Department of Education. (2005). *Estimated school dropout rates*. Retrieved June 18, 2006, from www.sde.state.ed.us/Finance/statistical.asp

Idaho State Department of Education. (2006). *Student ethnicity*. Retrieved June 18, 2006, from www.sde.state.id.us/Finance/ethnic.asp

Israel, E. (2005). News and trends. *Scholastic Instructor, 144*(6).

Janosz, M., LeBlanc, M., Boulerice, B., & Tremblay, R. E. (1997). Disentangling the weight of school dropout predictors: A test on two longitudinal samples. *Journal of Youth and Adolescence, 26*(6), 733+. Retrieved December 7, 2004, from www.idoc.state.id.us

Jehlen, A. (2003, March). High stakes questions. *NEA Today*, 8–11.

Jimerson, S., Anderson, G., & Whipple, A. (2002). Winning the battle and losing the war: Examining the relation between grade retention and dropping out of high school. *Psychology in the Schools, 39*(4), 441–457.

Jordan, W., McPartland, J., & Lara, J. (1999). Rethinking the causes of high school dropout. In S. Ungerleider (Ed.), *The Prevention Researcher, 6*(3), 33–36.

Kagel, S. (1995). Sexual identification and gender identity among father-absent males. *Sex Roles, 13*(5), 357–370. Retrieved May 15, 2005, from the Academic Search Premier database.

Kaminski, K. (1993). Rural dropouts: A causal comparison. *Education, 113*(4), 532+. Retrieved December 7, 2004, from www.questia.com

Kaufman, P. (2001). Dropping out of high school. In T. Urdan & F. Pajares (Eds.), *Adolescents and Education: Vol. 1.* Greenwich, CN: Information Age.

Kaufman, P., Alt, M., & Chapman, C. (2004). *Dropout rates in the United States: 2001* (NCES 2005–046). U.S. Department of Education. National Center for Education Statistics. Washington, DC: U.S. Government Printing Office.

Kerr, M. H., Beck, K., Shattuck, T. D., Kattar, C., & Uriburu, D. (2003). Family involvement: Problem and prosocial behavior outcomes of Latino youth. *American Journal of Health Behavior, 27*(Suppl. 1).

Knapp, M. S. (1995). *Teaching for meaning in high-poverty classrooms.* New York: Teachers College Press.

Knowledge loom. *Culturally responsive teaching.* Retrieved June 18, 2006, from http://knowledgeloom.org/crt/index.jsp

Kozol, J. (1991). *Savage inequalities: Children in America's schools.* New York: Crown.

Kozol, J. (2005, September). Still separate, still unequal: America's educational apartheid. *Harper's Magazine, 311*(1864), 41–54.

Ladson-Billings, G. (1994a). But that's just good teaching! The case for culturally relevant pedagogy. *Theory Into Practice, 34*(3), 159–165.

Ladson-Billings, G. (1994b). *The dreamkeepers: Successful teachers of African-American children.* San Francisco: Jossey-Bass.

Ladson-Billings, G. (1995). Toward a theory of culturally relevant pedagogy. *American Educational Research Journal, 32*, 465–491.

Ladson-Billings, G. (2006). 2006 presidential address. From the achievement gap to the education debt: Understanding achievement in U.S. schools. *Educational Researcher, 35*(7), 3–12.

Laezman, R. (2005). *100 Hispanic Americans who changed history.* New York: World Almanac History.

Landsman, J., & Lewis, C. (2006). *White teachers / diverse classrooms: A guide to building inclusive schools, promoting high expectations, and eliminating racism.* Sterling, VA: Stylus.

Larson, K., & Rumberger, R. W. (1999). Dropout prevention for highest risk Latino students. In S. Ungerleider (Ed.), *The Prevention Researcher*, 6(3), 39–41.

Lee, V. E., & Burkham, D. T. (2003). Dropping out of high school: The role of school organization and culture. *American Education Research Journal*, 40(2), 353–393.

Leeman, Y. (2003). School leadership for intercultural education. *Intercultural Education*, 14, 1.

Lehr, C., Johnson, D., Bremer, C., Cosio, A., & Thompson, M. (2004). *Essential Tools. Increasing rates of school completion: Moving from policy and research to practice*. Minneapolis, MN: ICI Publications Office.

Lichtenstein, G. (2003). *A call for high school reform*. Denver: Colorado Children's Campaign.

Llagas, C. (2003). Status and trends in the education of Hispanics (National Center for Education Statistics 2003–008). Washington, DC: U.S. Department of Education, Institute of Education Sciences.

Lockwood, A., & Secada, W. (1999). *Transforming education for Hispanic youth: Exemplary practices, programs and schools*. Retrieved December 12, 2005, from www.ncela.gwu.edu

Lopez, G. (2003a). Parent involvement as racialized performance. In G. Lopez & L. Parker (Eds.), *Interrogating racism in qualitative research methodology* (pp. 71–95). New York: Peter Lang.

Lopez, G. (2003b). The (racially neutral) politics of education: A critical race theory perspective. *Educational Administration Quarterly*, 39(1), 68–94.

Lunenburg, F. (2000). *High school dropouts: Issues and solutions*. Huntsville, TX: Sam Houston State University. (ERIC Document Reproduction Service No. ED448239)

MacLeod, J. (1987). *Ain't no makin' it: Leveled aspirations in a low-income neighborhood*. Boulder, CO: Westview Press.

Manning, L. M., & Baruth, L. G. (2000). *Multicultural education for children and adolescents*. (2nd ed.). Boston: Allyn & Bacon.

Marx, G. (2002, Spring). Ten trends: Educating children for tomorrow's schools. *Journal of School Improvement*, 3(1).

Marx, S. (2004). Regarding whiteness: Exploring and intervening in the effects of white racism in teacher education. *Equity & Excellence in Education*, 37, 31–43.

Maxwell, J. (1996). *Qualitative research design: An interactive approach*. Thousand Oaks, CA: Sage.

McPartland, J., & Jordan, W. (2004). Essential components of high school dropout-prevention reforms. In G. Orfield (Ed.), *Dropouts in America: Confronting the graduation rate crisis* (pp. 269–288). Cambridge, MA: Harvard Education Press.

Means, B., & Knapp , M. S. (1991). *Rethinking teaching for disadvantaged students: Teaching advanced skills to at-risk students.* San Francisco: Jossey-Bass.

Mehan, H. (1997). *Contextual factors surrounding Hispanic dropouts.* Retrieved September 12, 2004, from the Hispanic Dropout Project at UCSD Web site: http://create.ucsd.edu/Research_Evaluation/Contextual_Factors.htm

Menchaca, V., & Ruiz-Escalante, J. (1995). *Instructional strategies for migrant students.* Charleston, WV: ERIC/CRESS (ERIC Document Reproduction Service No. ED388491)

Merriam, S. (1998). *Qualitative research and case study applications in education.* San Francisco: Jossey-Bass.

Merriam, S. (Ed.). (2002). *Qualitative research in practice: Examples for discussion and analysis.* San Francisco: Jossey-Bass.

Miles, M., & Huberman, M. (1994). *Qualitative data analysis: An expanded sourcebook.* (2nd ed.). Thousand Oaks, CA: Sage.

Milian, M. (1999). Schools and family involvement: Attitudes among Latinos who have children with visual impairments. *Journal of Visual Impairment & Blindness, 93*(5), 277–291.

Mistral, G. [Lucila de Maria del Perpetuo Socorro Godoy Alcayaga]. (2003) *Selected poems of Gabriela Mistral* (U. K. LeGuin, Trans.). Albuquerque, NM: University of New Mexico Press.

Moustakas, C. (1994). *Phenomenological research methods.* Thousand Oaks, CA: Sage.

Moustakas, C. (1995). *Being-in, being-for, being-with.* Jason Aronson.

Nakkula, M. (2003). Identity and possibility: Adolescent development and the potential of schools. In M. Sadowski (Ed.), *Adolescents at school: Perspectives on youth, identity, and education.* Cambridge, MA: Harvard Education Press.

National Center for Children in Poverty. (2006, May). *The racial gap in parental education.* Factsheet. Retrieved June 16, 2006, from http://www.nccp.org

National Center for Education Statistics (NCES). (2007). *Urban/rural classification systems.* Retrieved July 2, 2007, from http://nces.ed.gov/surveys/RuralEd/definitions.asp

National Education Association. (2006a). *Minority community outreach. Teacher diversity: The need for a diverse teaching staff.* Retrieved November 20, 2006, from https://www.nea.org/mco/teacher.html

National Education Association. (2006b, May). *National teacher day spotlights key issues facing the profession.* Retrieved October 30, 2006, from http://www.nea.org/newsreleases/2006/nr060502.html

National Education Association. (2006c). *Nation's educators sound the alarm on school dropout crisis. NEA's plan for reducing the school dropout rate.*

Retrieved November 20, 2006, from http://www.nea.org/presscenter/actionplan1.html

National Study Group for the Affirmative Development of Academic Ability. (2004). *All students reaching the top: Strategies for closing academic achievement gaps* (ED-01–CO-0011). Naperville, IL: North Central Regional Educational Laboratory.

Nelson, A. (2006, Summer). Closing the gap: Keeping students in school. *Infobrief*, 46.

Nesman, T., Barobs-Gahr, B., & Medrano, L. (2001, April 2). *They are our kids: Significant findings from a 1998 Latino dropout study.* Paper presented at the National Migrant Education Conference, Orlando, Florida. (ERIC Document Reproduction Service No. ED459033)

Nieto, S. (2004). *Affirming diversity* (4th ed.). New York: Addison Wesley Longhorn.

No Child Left Behind Act of 2001. (2002). P.L. 107–110. Retrieved November 1, 2006, from http://www.ed.gov/nclb

Noddings, N. (1992). *The challenge to care in schools.* New York: Teachers College Press.

Noguera, P. (2003). *City schools and the American dream.* New York: Teachers College Press.

Obiakor, F. (2006). *Multicultural special education: Culturally responsive teaching.* Pearson Education.

Ogbu, J. (1987). Variability in minority school performance: A problem in search of an explanation. *Anthropology and Education Quarterly, 18*(4), 312–334.

Onikama, D., Hammond, O., & Koki, S. (n.d.). *Family involvement in education: A synthesis of research for Pacific educators.* Retrieved May 15, 2006, from http://www.prel.org/products/products/family-invol.htm

Orfield, G. (2001). *Schools more separate: Consequences of a decade of segregation.* Cambridge, MA: Civil Rights Project at Harvard University.

Orfield, G. (Ed.). (2004). *Dropouts in America: Confronting the graduation rate crisis.* Cambridge, MA: Harvard Education Press.

Orfield, G., Losen, D., Wald, J., & Swanson, C. B. (2004). Losing our future: How minority youth are being left behind by the graduation rate crisis. Retrieved January 12, 2005, from The Civil Rights Project at Harvard University Web site: www.civilrightsproject.ucla.edu

Osterling, J., & Garza, A. (2004). Strengthening Latino parental involvement: Forming community-based organizations/school partnership. *NABE Journal of Research and Practice, 2*(1). Retrieved December, 20, 2005, from http://njrp.tamu.edu/2004/PDFs/Osterling.pdf

Ovando, C. (2006, November 3). *Equity and excellence: Do we need to make a choice?* Presented to the annual meeting of the American Educational Studies Association, Butts Lecture, Spokane, WA.

Ovando, C., & McLaren, P. (2000). *The politics of multiculturalism and bilingual education: Students and teachers caught in the cross fire.* New York: McGraw-Hill Higher Education.

Pifer, D. A. (2000). Getting in trouble: The meaning of school for 'problem' students. *The Qualitative Report, 5,* 1–2. Retrieved August 16, 2004, from http://www.nova.edu.ssss/QR/QR5–1/pifer.html

Ramirez, A. (2003). Dismay and disappointment: Parental involvement of Latino immigrant parents. *The Urban Review, 35*(2), 93–110.

Reeves, C. (2003). Implementing the No Child Left Behind Act: Implications for rural schools and districts. *Educational Policy Publications.* Naperville, IL: North Central Regional Educational Lab. (ERIC Document Reproduction Service No. ED475037)

Riehl, C. (1999). Labeling and letting go: An organizational analysis of how high school students are discharged as dropouts. In A.M. Pallas (Ed.), *Research in Sociology of Education and Socialization.* Stanford, CN: JAI Press.

Riehl, C. (2000). The principal's role in creating inclusive schools for diverse students: A review of normative, empirical, and critical literature on the practice of educational administration. *Review of Educational Research, 70*(1), 55–81.

Robbins, K., Lindsey, R., Lindsey, D., & Terrell, R. (2002). *Culturally proficient instruction: A guide for people who teach.* Thousand Oaks, CA: Corwin Press.

Rodriguez, T. (2003). School social context on gender differences in academic achievement among second-generation Latinos. *Journal of Hispanic Higher Education, 2*(1), 332–333.

Romo, H. (1998). Latina high school leaving: Some practical solutions. *ERIC Digest.* Charleston, WV: ERIC/CRESS (ERIC Document Reproduction Service No. ED423096)

Romo, H., & Falbo, T. (1996). *Latino high school graduation: Defying the odds.* Austin, TX: University of Austin Press.

Rumberger, R. (1995). Dropping out of middle school: A multi-level analysis of students and schools. *American Educational Research Journal, 32*(3), 583–625.

Rumberger, R. (2001, January 13). *Why students drop out of school and what can be done.* Paper prepared for conference, Dropouts in America: How severe is the problem? What do we know about intervention and prevention? Harvard University. Retrieved May 12, 2004, from www.civilrightsproject.harvard.edu

Sadowski, M. (2003). Class and identity in a socioeconomically diverse high school: A discussion with Elaine Bessette, Joan Lowe, and Bill Quinn.

In M. Sadowski (Ed.), *Adolescents at school: Perspectives on youth, identity, and education.* Cambridge, MA: Harvard Education Press.

Salend, S., & Taylor, L. (1993). Working with families: A cross-cultural perspective. *Remedial and Special Education, 14*(5), 25–32.

Schmidt, P., & Ma, W. (2006). *50 literacy strategies for culturally responsive teaching, K-8.* Thousand Oaks, CA: Sage.

Schwartz, W. (1995). *School dropouts: New information about an old problem.* New York: ERIC Clearinghouse. (ERIC Document Reproduction Service No. ED386515)

Shabatay, V. (1991). The stranger's story: Who calls and who answers? In C. Wetherell & N. Noddings (Eds.), *Stories lives tell: Narrative and dialogue in education* (pp. 136–152). New York: Teachers College Press.

Smith, P. (2002). Raise a child, not a test score: Perspectives on bilingual education at Davis bilingual magnet school. *Bilingual Research Journal Online, 26*(1). Retrieved March 7, 2005, from http://brj.asu.edu/content/vol26_no1/abstracts.html

Sokolowski, R. (2000). *Introduction to phenomenology.* United Kingdom: Cambridge University Press.

Sosa, A. (1996). Involving Hispanic parents in improving educational opportunities for their children. San Antonio: University of Texas. (ERIC Document Reproduction Service No. ED393649)

Stanard, R. (2003). High school graduation rates in the United States: Implications for the counseling profession. *Journal of Counseling and Development, 81*(2), 217+. Retrieved December 7, 2004, from www.questia.com

Steele, C. (1997). A threat in the air: How stereotypes shape intellectual identities and performance. *American Psychologist, 52*(6), 613–629.

Swanson, C. B. (2003). *Keeping count and losing count: Calculation graduation rates for all students under NCLB accountability.* DC: Urban Institute.

Thompson, A. (1998). Not the color purple: Black feminist lessons for educational caring. *Harvard Educational Review, 68*(4), 522–554.

Thiederman, S. (2003). *Making diversity work: Seven steps for defeating bias in the workplace.* Chicago: Dearborn Trade Books.

Thornburgh, N. (2006). Dropout nation. *Time, 167*(16), 30–40.

Tiedt, P., & Tiedt, I. (2005). *Multicultural teaching: A handbook of activities, information and resources* (7th ed.). Boston: Pearson Education.

Tileston, D. W. (2005). *10 Best teaching practices: How brain research, learning styles, and standards define teaching competencies.* Thousand Oaks, CA: Corwin Press.

Tobias, S. (1990). *They're not dumb, they're different: Stalking the second tier.* Tucson, AZ: Research Corporation.

Tomlinson, C. (2003). *Fulfilling the promise of the differentiated classroom: Strategies and tools for responsive teaching.* Alexandria, VA: Association for Supervision & Curriculum Development.

Tomlinson, C., & McTighe, J. (2006). *Integrating differentiating instruction: Understanding by design.* Alexandria, VA: Association for Supervision and Curriculum Development.

Trueba, E., & Bartolome, L. (1997). The education of Latino students: Is school reform enough? *ERIC/CUE Digest, 123.* Retrieved May 17, 2006, from http://www.ed.gov/databases/ERIC_Digests/ed410367.htm

Trumbull, E., Rothstein-Fisch, C., Greenfield, P., & Quiroz, B. (2001). *Bridging cultures between home and school—A guide for teachers (with a special focus on Latino immigrant families).* Mahwah, NJ: Erbaum.

U.S. Census Bureau. (2000). *Census.* Retrieved November 22, 2004, from http://factfinder.census.gov

Valdes, G. (1996). *Con Respeto: Bridging the distances between culturally diverse families and schools: An ethnographic portrait.* New York: Teachers College Press.

Valenzuela, A. (1999). *Subtractive schooling: U.S.-Mexican youth and the politics of caring.* Albany: State University of New York Press.

Valverde, L., Borger, R. H., Haro, R., Baca, L., Acevedo, B., & Oritz, L. R. (2002). *A compromised commitment: Society's obligation and failure to serve the nation's largest growing population.* Tempe, AZ: Hispanic Border Leadership Institute, Arizona State University. (ERIC Document Reproduction Service No. ED464799)

Van Manen, M. (1990). *Researching lived experience: Human science for an action sensitive pedagogy.* Albany: The State University of New York Press.

Van Manen, M. (1996). Phenomenological pedagogy and the question of meaning. In D. Vandenberg (Ed.), *Phenomenology and Educational Discourse* (pp. 39–64). Durban, South Africa: Heinemann Higher and Further Education.

Van Manen, M. (2002). *Inquiry: Empirical methods.* Retrieved August 8, 2004, from http://www.phenomenologyonline.com

Verdugo, R. (2002). Race-ethnicity, social class, and zero-tolerance policies. *Education and Urban Society, 35*(1), 50–75.

Vogt, A. (2003). *Common courage: Bill Wassmuth, human rights, and small-town activism.* Moscow: University of Idaho Press.

Wehlage, G. (1989). *Reducing the risk: Schools as communities of support.* New York: Falmer Press.

Weiner, L., Leighton, N., & Funkhouse, J. (2000) *Using family and community resources in helping Hispanic students reach high academic standards:*

An idea book. Washington DC: Department of Education. (ERIC Document Reproduction Service No. 449263)

Wells, S. E. (1999). *At risk youth: Identification, programs, and recommendations.* Englewood, CO: Teacher Ideas Press.

Williams, P. (1997). *Seeing a color-blind future: The paradox of race.* New York: Noonday Press.

Witherell, C., & Noddings, N. (Eds.). (1991). *Stories lives tell: Narrative and dialogue in education.* New York: Teachers College Press.

Wlodkowski, R., & Ginsberg, M. (2003). *Diversity and motivation: Culturally responsive teaching.* Indianapolis, IN: John Wiley & Sons.

Wolff, R. (1999). A phenomenological study of in-church and televised worship. *Journal for the Scientific Study of Religion, 38*(2), 219–235.

Worthen, V. E. (2002). Phenomenological research and the making of meaning. In S. B. Merriam (Ed.), *Qualitative research in practice: Examples for discussion and analysis.* San Francisco: Jossey-Bass.

A Phenomenology

Previous researchers have looked at the problem of Latino/a dropouts, but these studies have largely focused on quantitative measures, such as graduation rates. Much of the literature focused on the fact that Latino/a students are dropping out at a disproportionate rate when compared to White and African American students, and on characteristics of dropouts, in an effort to identify them as at-risk and provide intervention. However, reform measures to date have been ineffective in lowering Latino/a dropout rates.

Qualitative studies with high school students and dropouts have revealed, to an extent, the reasons students give for dropping out and the characteristics of a high school dropout. In a phenomenological study focused on three alternative school students and the meaning of school for them, Pifer (2000) found that in-depth perspectives of students are missing from the literature: studies that "present the voices of students explicating their perceptions, and specifically the voices of students constructed in 'outsider' roles" are needed (p. 27). From our collective experience as educators we were convinced that listening to the individual stories of rural, Latina/o students who have experienced the phenomenon of school dropout would be valuable.

Phenomenology is a research tradition that focuses on how people interpret everyday experiences from the perspective of meaning it has for them.

> The object of phenomenological research is to "borrow" other people's experiences. We gather other people's experiences because they allow us, in a vicarious sort of way, to become more experienced ourselves . . . they allow us to become informed, shaped, or enriched by this experience so as to be able to render the full significance of its meaning. (Van Manen, 2002, p. 17)

This phenomenological investigation was guided by the researchers Giorgi (1985), Moustakas (1994), Sokolowski (2000), and Van Manen (1990, 1996, and 2002). The research focused on the lived experience for Latina/o dropouts from rural high schools and the meaning they attached to the dropout phenomenon. Participants were interviewed at least twice. Spending extended time in the field was employed to get the rich data needed to successfully complete this study.

The purpose of this phenomenological study was to explore what it means to be a Latina/o dropout from a rural community in the context of the No Child Left Behind Act, and to describe that experience so that those who read the account would gain insight into their world. In qualitative inquiry, the intent is not to generalize findings to a population, but instead to develop exploration of a central phenomenon.

THEORETICAL SENSITIVITY

The study was engaged from a phenomenological perspective, with a focus on understanding how people make sense of their lives and their experiences (Moustakas, 1994, 1995; Sokolowski, 2000). Theoretical sensitivity came primarily from the research method of phenomenology, which requires that researchers bracket preconceived ideas or judgment and maintain an ongoing skepticism regarding logical understandings of the phenomenon to stay open to the authentic voices of participants. The goal was to allow the description, analysis, and interpretation of the experience to come from the voices of the participants themselves.

The accounts that we provide contain many direct quotes from participants so that the reader becomes intimate with their thoughts, desires and emotions. The lives of the students in and out of school become real, for instance, Silvia's emotion when she said, "People at school just didn't want me to succeed, so I always felt angry about it. For me, nobody was going to admit that there were hazing or harassment problems in the school." Similarly, when Victor explained what was going on at home that interfered with his schooling, his perspective made sense and selling marijuana was a practical outcome in a dire situation: "My brother was hungry yesterday and I had some money so I took both of my brothers to eat. My sister didn't want to eat, and my mom didn't. I just do whatever I can because I feel sorry for them because my dad's not there. The refrigerator is empty, and their clothes are from last year. As soon as I get a job I'm going to buy both my brothers some clothes. Who else is going to do it?"

We sought to remain open to the voices of participants, but our own prior and current experiences as educators and the literature also informed the study. We have included a sample of some of these biases, interests, and assumptions in Chapter 2. Three key areas of research also gave us ways to look at the data. First, the literature on school dropouts that acknowledged that schools reproduce educational and social inequity and that students drop out of school after continual problems with school authorities was useful (Fine, 1991; Rumberger, 2001). Research suggested that high schools reject students by adopting policies that exclude them from extracurricular participation, detentions that do not involve school-related work, and suspensions, all factors that make it easier for students to become disengaged (Fine, 1991; Rumberger, 2001). Similarly, Romo and Falbo (1996) argued that Latina/o families value education highly, yet students are discouraged by school policies and practices, such as tracking and grade retention.

Second, critical race theory and Latino critical race theory drew attention to how the dominant literature often unfairly attributed school failure to individual and/or personal characteristics of Latino/a students and their families and discounted external and social factors (Lopez, 2003a, p. 87; 2003b). In the dominant literature, Latina/o students have been portrayed as withdrawn and sullen in nature, as well as low achievers in the classroom (e.g., see Kagel, 1995). This literature failed to take into account classism and racism in the larger society and in the school contexts and experiences. Studies such as those from Ceja (2004) and Trueba and Bartolome (1997) noted that those operating from a cultural deficit model reinforce the myth that parenting styles, language barriers, and the focus upon securing income are causal factors for low educational attainment and the dropout rate of Latino/a youth.

Third, culturally relevant literature on multicultural education and social justice gave specific strategies for principals and teachers to foster a culture of inclusion and success for all students. For example, Gay stated, "decontextualizing teaching and learning from the ethnicities and cultures of students minimizes the chances that their achievement potential will ever be fully realized" (2000, p. 23).

HOW DEPENDABLE, CREDIBLE, AND TRANSFERABLE IS OUR STUDY?

Dependability

Dependability, auditability, and trustworthiness are terms that apply to phenomenological research instead of the quantitative term of reliability because the study and its results cannot be replicated. "The question is not whether findings will be found again, but whether the results are consistent with the data collected" (Merriam, 1998, p. 206). We sought dependability, auditability, and trustworthiness through a variety of steps, including having multiple researchers, keeping an audit trail (or complete record of the research process), and employing triangulation (using multiple and different sources: students, teachers, parents, and probation officers).

Credibility and Transferability

Internal validity deals with the question of how closely research findings match reality. We do not use this term because we recognize multiple realities, and so instead use the term, credibility. We provided rich detail and the context of the study and its participants to seek credibility. Merriam (1998) reminded researchers that because humans are the primary instrument of data collection and analysis in qualitative research, the researcher gets a closer view of reality than if a data collection instrument had been used. Credibility refers to the degree to which the researcher's claim to knowledge corresponds to the research participant's constructions of reality. "In accordance with phenomenological principles, scientific investigation is valid when the knowledge sought is arrived at through descriptions that make possible an understanding of the meanings and essences of experiences" (Moustakas, 1994, p. 84). Giorgi (1985) provided a concrete example of analyzing interview respondent text through the description, reduction, essences, intentionality processes. The following description demonstrates the rigor behind a phenomenological study that holds up to questions about internal validity.

> The method contains four essential steps, expressed most generally they are as follows: (1) One reads the entire description in order to get a general sense of the whole statement. (2) Once the sense of the whole has been grasped, the researcher goes back to the beginning and reads through the text once more with the specific aim of discriminating 'meaning units' from within a psychological perspective and with a focus on the phenomenological aspect being researched. (3) Once "meaning units" have been delineated, the researcher then goes through all the meaning units and expresses the psychological insight contained in them more directly. (4) Finally, the researcher synthesizes all of the transformed meaning units into a consistent statement regarding the subject's experience. (p. 10)

The researcher must also be fully aware and understand how personal bias and values influence the conduct and conclusions of the study. Explaining the researcher's own values, interests, and purposes is critical.

Another issue is participant reactivity in interviews because what the participant discloses is always a function of both the interviewer and the interview (Maxwell, 1996). Consequently, we employed the following techniques suggested by seasoned researchers to help improve the rigor of the study (J. Creswell, 1998; Maxwell, 1996; Merriam, 1998; Miles & Huberman, 1994; Moustakas, 1994):

- "Rich" data: extensive verbatim transcripts of the interviews
- Triangulation (the use of a variety of theories and research methods)
- Feedback from a variety of people who are familiar with the phenomenon or setting under study, and also from those who are not
- Long-term or repeated observations
- Clarification of researcher biases, assumptions, worldview, and theoretical orientation
- Member checks: soliciting feedback about data and conclusions from the people who are under study

Finally, external validity is also a term that is not used in phenomenological research because generalization is not possible, given the differences in times and places. However, in this study, we did seek transferability. We followed the process of Miles and Huberman (1994), and self-consciously collected and double-checked our findings using multiple sources and modes of evidence to build confirmation. We carefully retained, in easily retrievable forms, all study materials, from raw field notes through data displays and final text. Also important was a reflexive stance to the conduct of the study that "assumes regular, on-going, self-conscious documentation—of successive versions of coding schemes, of analysis episodes—both successful and dead end ones" (p. 439). In the final product we sought to describe the experiences of dropping out of school and the sense-making and wisdom that each participant brought to that experience.

Portraits of the Latino/a youth who dropped out of school and our theory that arose from the data—that they were seeking satisfaction given a negative experience in school—were presented in fine detail. We were ever cognizant of our responsibility to conduct a dependable, credible study. The reader will decide whether the findings are transferable. Our work was to provide a thorough and personal study of the lives and school experiences of nine individuals attending six schools (three high schools and three alternative high schools) in three communities in rural Idaho.

APPENDIX B

Interview Guides

1. Tell a little about yourself (age, last grade completed, hobbies, and interests).
2. Tell what you do with your time now that you are not in school.
3. Describe your family and background.
4. How do your parents view your education?
5. What are typical statements made by your parents about school and education?
6. What are your parents' expectations for you regarding high school?
7. What about after high school?
8. What are your beliefs about education?
9. Do you believe that it is important to graduate from high school in order to be successful in life?
10. Do you believe you have an equal chance with Whites to get ahead through education?
11. Finish this sentence for me: I was the student who . . .
12. Describe your school experience so far (kindergarten to now).
13. What experiences about school stand out as memorable (positive and negative).
14. What does it mean to be a student in this community?
15. What difficulties have you had in school? Why?
16. Were you ever held back one or more grades? Tell me about that.
17. Did you ever move or change schools? Tell me about that.

18. Tell me about the best teacher you ever had and why he or she was good.
19. Tell me about the worst teacher you ever had and why he or she was not good.
20. How could the school(s) have been more supportive of you?
21. What do you know about the student testing portion of the No Child Left behind Act? Did you ever take the ISAT tests? How did you do?
22. How did taking the tests make you feel?
23. What questions have I not asked that I should ask to learn more about why students drop out of school?
24. Any other comments or ideas?

INTERVIEW 2

1. Tell me more about [a follow-up question from the first interview].
2. When you were back in grade school, what did you say you wanted to be when you grew up? What changed for you?
3. When did you first become aware that you were actually going to drop out of high school?
4. Describe the day you decided to drop out. What was it like? What was said and by whom? What were you feeling?
5. What do you say to people who ask about dropping out?
6. Do you say the same thing to older adults as you say to people in your own age group?
7. Are there different answers for different people? Explain that to me.
8. What thoughts do you have about missing school dances or other school events?
9. What thoughts do you have about missing graduating with your classmates?
10. What about down the road—the high school reunion. What thoughts do you have about that event?
11. If you listen to music, read poetry or books, or watch movies, are there particular words either that remind you of your experience of dropping out or that bring you comfort?
12. If you could rewind this experience, what would you do differently?

13. What would you not change?
14. What would you say your life project is now? What are your future plans?
15. Have you ever thought about getting a GED or high school equivalency certificate?
16. How do you think other people define what a dropout is?
17. What do you tell yourself about the experience of dropping out?
18. What does it mean to you to be called a dropout?
19. What would you say to teachers, school leaders, and lawmakers that would help them understand what this experience of not graduating from high school means?
20. What advice would you have for students who are in the early grades?
21. What advice would you have for students who are in the middle grades?
22. What advice would you have for high school students who are considering dropping out of school?
23. What do you regret or are disappointed about regarding your school experiences?
24. What memories satisfy you in regard to your school experiences?
25. What achievements are you most proud of?

Thank you so much for helping me to understand your experience.

APPENDIX C

Recommendations for Superintendents and Policy Makers

1. Include Latino/a issues in college and district-level master planning, and tie master planning to the budget.
2. Implement a consistent district, state, and nationwide record-keeping system that will allow comparable state high school completion and dropout data to be reported on a regular basis.
3. Support and monitor Latino/a students from the earliest grade levels. It is imperative that possible disengagement from school be identified at an early age and prevented through careful attention to high expectations to ensure that children have success in school.
4. Work with media organizations, such as local radio stations, to ensure that school information is broadcast in Spanish and English to families.
5. Develop strategies that support the goal that all public schools, regardless of their locations, are funded equitably.
6. Know the legal rights (federal and state) of all populations of students to effective education, and the legal responsibilities of the educational institutions to provide effective programs.
7. Disseminate information to teachers, administrators, and institutions on the law and about all populations of students (English Language Learners, Limited English Proficient, special education).
8. Adopt an explicit state policy of local control and flexibility in creating programs to meet the needs of English Language Learners.

9. Provide focused culturally responsive professional development for school administrators as well as other staff (teachers, counselors) in order to guide Limited English Proficient (LEP) educational programs effectively. Indeed, as mentioned earlier in this book, we prefer the term that Gonzales (2002) used, PEP, Potentially English Proficient, to signify high expectations and confidence in the learner rather than a deficiency status.

10. Provide professional development in second language acquisition for all administrators, teachers, and counselors.

11. Cultivate relationships with Latino/a community leaders and parents. Establish the concept of *mi escuela* (my school). Schools need to become more like communities where students gain a sense of belonging, and parents and teachers have a strong sense of joint ownership.

12. Assess English proficiency when the student enters the school system and keep records of periodic assessment thereafter. Teachers should be kept up-to-date about state-of-the-art strategies for language instruction specifically, and for instruction generally, that accounts for students' varying levels of English proficiency. Teachers should disseminate any promising practices for ELL students.

13. Give incentives to teachers to provide a combination of native language instruction and instruction in English for LEP/PEP students. Administrators should provide professional development on ESL, and sheltered techniques.

14. Encourage and reward administrators, staff, and students who are bilingual and multilingual.

15. Encourage parents and students to use Spanish and English at home to preserve the first culture, language, and literature. For second- and third-generation Latina/os, offer Spanish language classes, but do not assume all will take this opportunity, as they may prefer to speak English only. It may take another generation to realize what has been lost in the assimilation process and for acculturation (adding on another culture) and Spanish language fluency to be seen as a valuable asset.

16. Recruit, hire, mentor, promote, and retain Latino/a teachers, administrators, special educators, and counselros, particularly those who are bilingual and bi-literate. Offer stipends where needed to encourage Latino/as to enter the educational field.

17. Make provisions to allow for reduced class sizes for PEP/LEP students.

18. Implement a more powerful curriculum and instruction by providing professional development on culturally responsive schooling that connects with the needs and interest of Latino/a students.

19. Establish remediation and tutorial programs. (For a variety of program suggestions, see Lehr, Johnson, Bremer, Cosio, & Thompson, 2004; Lunenburg, 2000; McPartland & Jordan, 2004).

20. Revise funding mechanisms so that schools will be rewarded for helping students rapidly attain English proficiency.

21. Design and support research that informs educators and the public of the aspects of students' experiences that determine whether these students complete secondary school.

22. Develop state policy requiring each school system to establish a management information system (MIS) that provides basic and common data on all students.

23. Retain administrators with expertise in culturally responsive leadership to provide leadership in educating Latino/a students.

24. Obtain board, administrative, and community support for increasing funding in the areas of need for Latino/a students.

25. Increase budgetary support at the individual, local, state, and federal levels for vocational programs, financial aid, language curricula, and other culturally responsive and multicultural programs.

26. Re-examine local policies and practices regarding the General Education Diploma (GED), which requires no school attendance or participation but has one requirement: the ability to pass the written test. School personnel often promote the GED for students at risk of dropping out, and students can see the GED as an alternative to high school completion. However, if educators were knowledgeable about the GED, they might be more inclined to counsel students to stay in school. Educators themselves do not always understand the difficulty of the test. Taking the GED requires (a) self-motivation; (b) the ability to pay for the tests; (c) frequent tutoring, which can be expensive; and (d) access to GED testing centers, which may require considerable travel from the communities in which many rural students live. These are all further obstacles for rural Latino/a youth, especially because the GED does not always benefit youth who do not intend to go on to college. However, the GED was the means that allowed Yolanda access to education,

and she is now highly educated. GED programs can be a valuable reentry to education and must be supported and expanded. School administrators must work with state GED services, High School Equivalency (HEP) programs, and universities to promote access to further education and careers.

Cultural Responsiveness in Standards for School Leaders

1. Visionary and Strategic Leadership
   - A written culturally responsive leadership plan developed by diverse constituents
   - Diverse administrators, faculty, staff, students, and board members
   - Culturally responsive teaching, school policies, and practices
   - School and district cultures that affirm diversity
   - High expectations for all
2. Instructional Leadership
   - Incorporation of community diversity into educational programs
   - Appreciation for the variety of ways students can learn
   - Language, culture, and literacy programs
   - Multicultural and culturally relevant curriculum and assessment
   - Restructured curriculum to engage all students
   - Professional development offered in antiracism, inclusion, and diversity
3. Management and Organizational Leadership
   - Safe, efficient, and effective learning environment
   - Communication skills (across racial, ethnic, and cultural differences)
   - Provision of a supportive environment affirming diversity
   - Awareness of racism and implementation of proactive strategies of antiracism
4. Family and Community Partnerships
   - Collaborative partnerships with families and community
   - Agenda for social and educational change
   - Affirmation of home cultures

5. Professional and Ethical Leadership
   - Learning-centered leadership
   - Understanding of diverse values
   - Appreciation for principles in the Bill of Rights
   - Caring school climate
   - Mentoring networks
   - Prevention programs in early childhood years against school failure
   - Positive teacher-student interactions and organizational climate
   - High expectations and appropriate, engaging curriculum and teaching methods
6. Governance and Legal Leadership
   - Understanding of the larger social context and the importance of diversity and equity in a democratic society
   - Engagement of representatives of diverse community groups with schools
   - Business and university collaboration
   - Alternatives to traditional schooling
   - High-achieving schools with equitable outcomes for all groups of students

(Adapted from Idaho Foundation Standards for School Leaders, 2007)

Resources for Culturally Responsive Teaching and Leadership

Ableza. *Appropriate methods when teaching about Native American peoples*. Retrieved June 25, 2006, from http://www.ableza.org/dodont.html

A Class Divided. (2003). PBS Frontline presentation. Retrieved July 2, 2007, from http://www.pbs.org/wgbh/pages/frontine/shows/divided

African American history. Retrieved June 18, 2006, from http://www.watson.org/~lisa/blackhistory/

Afrocentric Experience. *Black Inventors*. Retrieved July 27, 2006, from http://www.swagga.com/inventors.htm

AISNE guide to hiring and retaining teachers of color. Retrieved June 19, 2006, from http://www.aisne.org/member_services/services/diversity_services.asp

Bilingual Research Journal. Retrieved June 18, 2006, from http://brj.asu.edu

BKFK. Bykidsforkids. *Famous Hispanic inventors*. Retrieved July 27, 2006, from http://www.bkfk.com/inventions/hispanic.asp

Carr Center for Human Rights Policy. Harvard University. Retrieved June 18, 2006, from http://www.ksg.harvard.edu/cchrp/

Center for Applied Linguistics. *Directory of two-way bilingual immersion programs*. Retrieved June 19, 2006, from http://www.cal.org/

Center for Multicultural Education, University of Washington. Retrieved June 18, 2006, from http://depts.washington.edu/centerme/home.htm

Center for Racial Sensitivity. Dr. Keith L. Anderson. keithanderson@idaho-crs.com; keithanderson@keithlanderson.com Retrieved June 21, 2006, from http://www.Idaho-crs.com

Center for the Study of White American Culture. A site examining White privilege and promoting antiracism. Retrieved June 18, 2006, from http://www.euroamerican.org

Child Trends Data Bank. Retrieved June 19, 2006, from http://www.childtrendsdatabank.org/index.cfm

Contributions of American Indians and Alaska Natives to American Life. Floy C. Pepper. Retrieved June 25, 2006, from http://www.kidsource.com/kidsource/content3/unbiased.teaching.k12.2.html

Culturally Responsive Teaching. Retrieved June 18, 2006, from http://www.intime.uni.edu/multiculture/curriculum/culture/Teaching.htm

Culturally Responsive Teaching. Retrieved November 2, 2006, from http://www.lab.brown.edu/tdl/tl-strategies/crt-principles-prt.shtml

EdChange. *Multicultural pavilion.* Paul C. Gorski. Retrieved June 18, 2006, from http://www.edchange.org/multicultural/

EdChange Multicultural Pavillion. Retrieved June 21, 2006, from http://www.edchange.org/multicultural/activityarch.html

Electronic magazine of multicultural education. Retrieved June 18, 2006, from http://www.eastern.edu/publications/emme/

Ethics Resource Center. *Statistics.* Retrieved June 19, 2006, from http://www.ethics.org/character/stats_poverty.html

Facing History and Ourselves. Lessons and units for grades 8–12. Retrieved June 19, 2006, from http://www.facinghistorycampus.org

Hispanic Outlook in Higher Education Magazine. Retrieved June 19, 2006, from http://www.hispanicoutlook.com/

Human Rights Education Association. Retrieved June 19, 2006, from http://www.hrea.org/

Idaho Human Rights Education Center. Retrieved June 18, 2006, from http://www.idaho-humanrights.org

Idaho Kids Count. *2005 data book.* Statistics on family and community in Idaho (other states have similar data reports). Retrieved June 18, 2006, from http://www.idahokidscount.org/

Interactive Cultural Diversity Program. *Freshmen learn about diversity at "Ba Fa Ba Fa."* D. Heimburger. Retrieved October 31, 2006, from http://www-tech.mit.edu/V118/N33/diversity.33n.html

Knowledge Loom. *Culturally responsive teaching.* Retrieved June 18, 2006, from http://knowledgeloom.org/crt/index.jsp

Learning Disabilities Association of America. Retrieved June 19, 2006, from http://www.ldanatl.org/

Legal responsibilities of education agencies serving language minority students. Retrieved June 19, 2006, from http://www.maec.org/legal.html

Lonely Planet. This is a commerce site that includes travel and cultural information on many countries. Retrieved June 21, 2006, from http://www.lonelyplanet.com/

Multicultural education and ethnic groups: Selected internet sources. Paul Gorski and Bob Covert. Retrieved June 18, 2006, from http://www.library.csustan.edu/lboyer/multicultural/main.htm

Multicultural education internet resource guide. Dr. Jon Reyner. Retrieved June 18, 2006, from http://jan.ucc.nau.edu/~jar/Multi.html

National Association of Bilingual Education (NABE). Retrieved June 18, 2006, from http://www.nabe.org

National Association for Multicultural Education: Advocates for Educational Equity and Social Justice. Retrieved June 18, 2006, from http://www.nameorg.org/

National Association for the Advancement of Colored People. Retrieved June 18, 2006, from http://www.naacp.org/

National Center for Education Statistics. U.S. Department of Education. (2003). *Condition of Education.*

National Center for Children in Poverty. Retrieved June 18, 2006, from http://www.nccp.org

National Center for Culturally Responsive Educational Systems. Retrieved June 18, 2006, from http://www.nccrest.org/

National Center on Secondary Education and Transition. *Creating opportunities for youth with disabilities to achieve successful futures.* The NCSET has published a manual, *Essential tools. Increasing rates of school completion: Moving from policy and research to practice.* Retrieved June 19, 2006, from www.ncset.org

National Clearinghouse for English Language Acquisition (NCELA), with publications. Retrieved June 19, 2006, from http://www.ncela.gwu.edu/

National Council of La Raza. *Making a difference for Hispanic Americans.* Retrieved June 18, 2006, from http://www.nclr.org/

National Dropout Prevention Centers. See the Coca Cola Valued Youth Program: Across-age tutoring program that takes older students who are considered at risk of dropping out and places them, with ongoing training, as tutors of younger students. Results show it as a highly effective program. Retrieved June 19, 2006, from http://www.dropout-prevention.org

National Society for Hispanic Professionals. NSHP. Retrieved July 27, 2006, from http://www.nshp.org/

New Horizons for Learning. *Multicultural education.* Mary Stone Hanley. Includes articles from noted researchers that can be downloaded and printed. Retrieved June 18, 2006, from http://www.newhorizons.org/strategies/multicultural/front_multicultural.htm

North Central Regional Educational Laboratory. *Culturally responsive education.* Retrieved June 18, 2006, from http://www.ncrel.org/sdrs/areas/issues/students/learning/lr1cre.htm

North Central Regional Educational Laboratory. *Multicultural education.* Retrieved June 18, 2006, from http://www.ncrel.org/sdrs/areas/issues/educatrs/presrvce/pe3lk1.htm

NW Regional Educational Laboratory. *Developmentally appropriate and culturally responsive education: Theory in practice.* Prepared by Rebecca Novick. Retrieved June 18, 2006, from http://www.nwrel.org/cfc/publications/DAP2.html

People's Institute for Survival and Beyond. *Undoing Racism.* Retrieved November 1, 2006, from http://www.pisab.org/about-us/

Race Relations. A commerce site, but with interesting links and information. Retrieved June 18, 2006, from http://asianamculture.about.com/

Reach. A site for Spanish teachers, Spanish-speaking students in the United States, and the general public. Retrieved June 21, 2006, from http://www.nflc.org/REACH/

Resource guide for parents and teachers on adoption as part of a school curriculum. Retrieved June 19, 2006, from http://www.fairfamilies.org

Robins Group. *Organizational development: Leadership, change, diversity and spirituality.* Retrieved June 18, 2006, from http://www.kikanza-nurirobins.com/events.htm

The Southern Poverty Law Center. *Teaching tolerance.* Provides materials, resources, and multicultural resources for classrooms. Many resources (books, posters, videotapes, etc.) are provided to schools free when requested on school letterhead. Retrieved June 18, 2006, from http://www.tolerance.org/

Teaching diverse learners: Equity and excellent for all. Retrieved June 18, 2006, from http://www2.alliance.brown.edu/tdl/tl-strategies/crt-principles.shtml

Teaching for inclusion. Retrieved June 18, 2006, from http://ctl.unc.edu/tfi5.html

Teacher Talk. A publication that includes articles and ideas on multiculturalism. Retrieved June 18, 2006, from http://education.indiana.edu/cas/tt/tthmpg.html

Teachers of English to Speakers of Other Languages (TESOL). Retrieved June 19, 2006, from http://www.tesol.org/

Web sites for students of Spanish. Includes Hispanic cultural knowledge. Retrieved June 18, 2006, from http://www.spanish.sbc.edu/Language_Sites.html

Working to Improve Schools and Education (WISE). *Multicultural education and culturally responsive teaching.* Retrieved June 18, 2006, from http://www.ithaca.edu/wise/topics/multicultural.htm

APPENDIX F

Professional Development Activities for Cultural Responsiveness

ACTIVITY 1: SMALL GROUP DISCUSSION
Knowing Your Colleagues (EDChange Multicultural Pavillion)

OBJECTIVES: (1) Participants will get to know the names of each person in the class, group, or community, as well as something about each person's background. (2) Participants will have a greater understanding and appreciation for the diversity within the group, while realizing that they have things in common with some of the people they have felt most removed from.

ACTIVITY DESCRIPTION: Participants should sit in a circle for this exercise, if possible. Facilitator should hand out a list of questions for each participant. Before you begin the exercise, instruct the participants to identify one or two people in the group whom they do not know well, and to think about what answers they expect feom those people after they have written their own responses. This part will not be shared among group members, but can help people realize how they formulate ideas about people based on appearance. Give participants time to write. Tell the group that each person will be given about two minutes. The facilitator should begin in order to model the kind of information that should be shared. Remind participants that they only have to reveal what they feel comfortable revealing. (Be sensitive to those who may not know about their heritage or who have been adopted.) Once everyone has had an opportunity to share their information, ask the group to discuss what they have learned from this exercise.

175

1. What is your nickname?
2. What is your ethnic background?
3. Where are you from?
4. Where were your parents born?
5. Which generation do you represent in America for your family?
6. What is one custom or tradition that your family practices?

ACTIVITY 2: JELLY BEAN EXERCISE
(Anderson, 2006, pp 150–151)

Place 20–30 jelly beans in a pile on the table in front of each participant: Red for Native Americans, Black for African Americans, Brown for Latinos, White for European Americans, Yellow for Asian Americans. The instructor reads the question and the participant places the colored jelly bean that represents their answer in a clear plastic bag. At the end of the exercise, participants reflect on the diversity present, or not present, in their lives and what that might mean in order to effectively serve all students and families.

Which jelly bean best represents . . .
Your lover, husband, or wife
Your lover, boyfriend, or girlfriend before your current one
Your best friend
Your boss
The majority of the people at your place of worship or social activity
Your neighbor to your right
Your neighbor to your left
Your son's or daughter's best friend
The last person you had lunch with
Your favorite historical person
The last visitor to eat at your dinner table (not a family member)
Your three favorite students

Index

177

Made in the USA
Lexington, KY
19 May 2011